CW01261438

REMEMBERING FRANCIS
Champion of the Environment

COMPILED BY SR JANET FEARNS FMDM

redemptorist
publications

PREFACE

Janet Fearns FMDM

Eight hundred years ago, in 1225, as St Francis of Assisi lay seriously ill, blind, months from death and in tremendous pain, he wrote *The Canticle of the Creatures*, also known as *The Canticle of Brother Sun*.

On 24 May 2015, Pope Francis used the words of his saintly namesake "Laudato si, mi Signore" "Praise be to you, my Lord" as the opening words of the first-ever Encyclical on the Environment.

Pope Francis used every opportunity to encourage the world to cherish Creation, often speaking out as a courageous prophet of behalf of our fragile "Sister Mother Earth", as St Francis called her.

In the following pages, St Francis and Pope Francis offer a shared plea to see God in all things. In the words of "the little poor man of Assisi", which Pope Francis echoed in all that he said and did:

"Praise and bless my Lord and give him thanks and serve him with great humility."

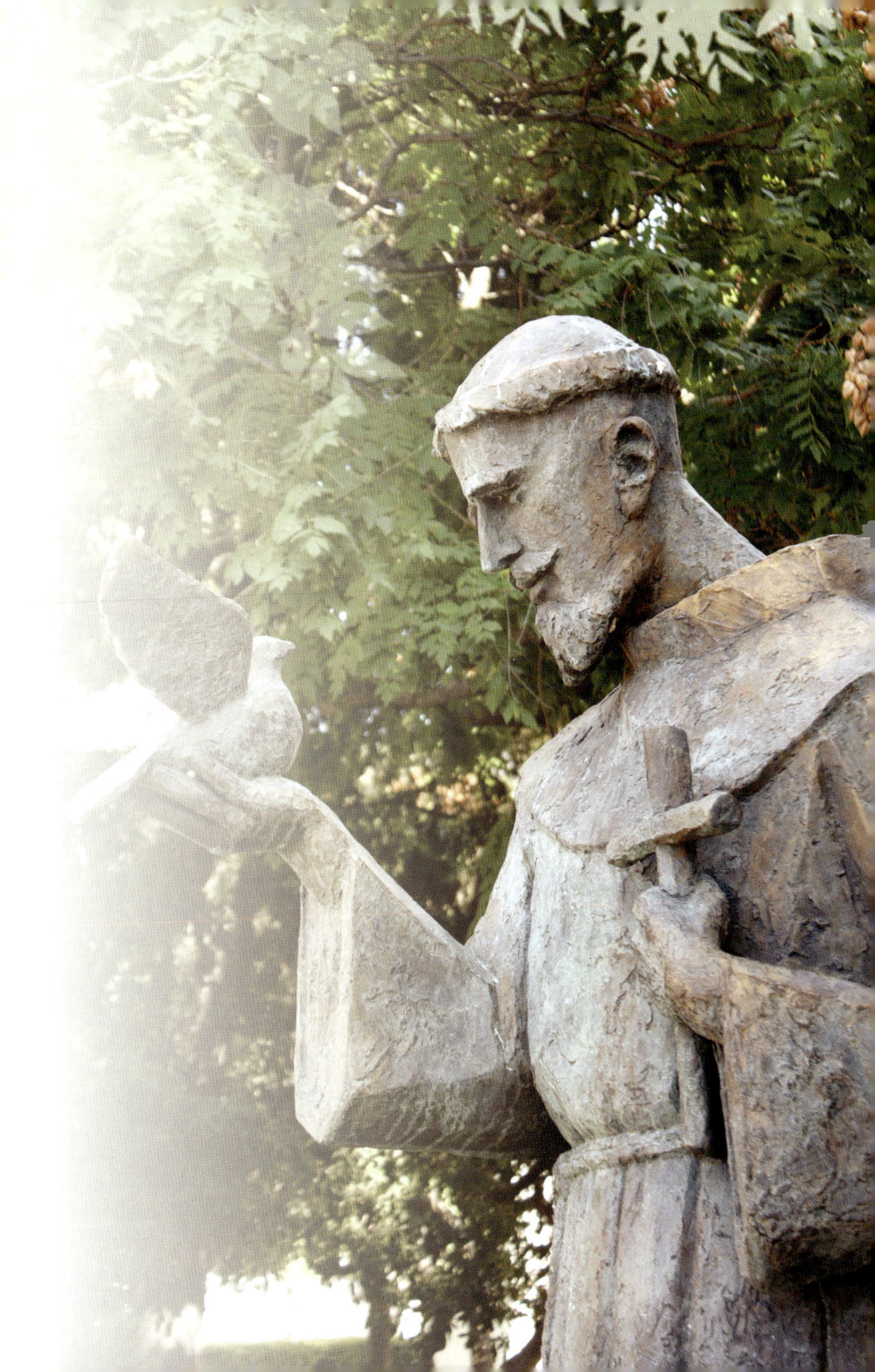

THE PEOPLE'S POPE

The tale (possibly apocryphal) is told of a bishop whose lifestyle had become noticeably simpler and more frugal. Asked the reason for the change, he smiled and said, "I've been Francised!"

From the very moment that Cardinal Jean-Louis Tauran appeared on the balcony of St Peter's and declared, "Habemus Papam", the newly elected Pope Francis did things differently. He greeted the vast crowd in St Peter's Square with a simple "Buona sera" ("Good evening"); he asked the people to bless him before he gave them his first papal blessing.

Francis declared: "I prefer a Church which is bruised, hurting and dirty because it has been out on the streets, rather than a Church which is unhealthy from being confined and from clinging to its own security." He wanted a Church in which "its shoes get soiled by the mud of the street." This longing sometimes created enemies as he tried to reform the Curia and make the Church more merciful and more compassionate. Yet Francis also inspired unswerving loyalty in the hearts of millions of people who saw him reach out to the reality of their own lives.

As with any reformer, Pope Francis was fearlessly controversial. Not everyone accepted his challenge to see the world differently. As with St Francis of Assisi, whose name he chose, Francis' concerns were for people who were poor, disadvantaged and marginalised. He proclaimed peace, mercy, compassion and care for Creation. He castigated power brokers and warmongers.

Francis was the first Pope to have been ordained after Vatican II, the first Jesuit Pope and the first from Latin America. An Argentinian laywoman declared, "If you want to understand Pope Francis, you have first to see him as a Latin American. Life has been so hard in Latin America that we are brought up to 'think outside the box' for our very survival. Francis brought this ability with him when he became Pope. He could do things differently because he had been trained to 'think outside the box.'"

Perhaps Francis' approach to his pontificate can be summarised in his own words: "I'm talking about getting involved in people's lives, I am talking about closeness. Talk little, listen a lot, say just enough, and always look people in the eye."

ALIVE AND WITH US ALWAYS

These were some of the very last words Pope Francis spoke to us, less than twenty-four hours before he went home to God. Even in his last hours, Pope Francis was echoing some of the final words of St Francis: "I have done what is mine to do; may Christ teach you what is yours."

Christ is risen. He is alive! He is no longer a prisoner of death, he is no longer wrapped in the shroud, and therefore we cannot confine him to a fairy tale, we cannot make him a hero of the ancient world or think of him as a statue in a museum! On the contrary, we must look for him and this is why we cannot remain stationary. We must take action, set out to look for him: look for him in life, look for him in the faces of our brothers and sisters, look for him in everyday business, look for him everywhere except in the tomb.

We must look for him without ceasing. Because if he has risen from the dead, then he is present everywhere. He dwells among us. He hides himself and reveals himself even today in the sisters and brothers we meet along the way, in the most ordinary and unpredictable situations of our lives. He is alive and is with us always, shedding the tears of those who suffer and adding to the beauty of life through the small acts of love carried out by each of us…

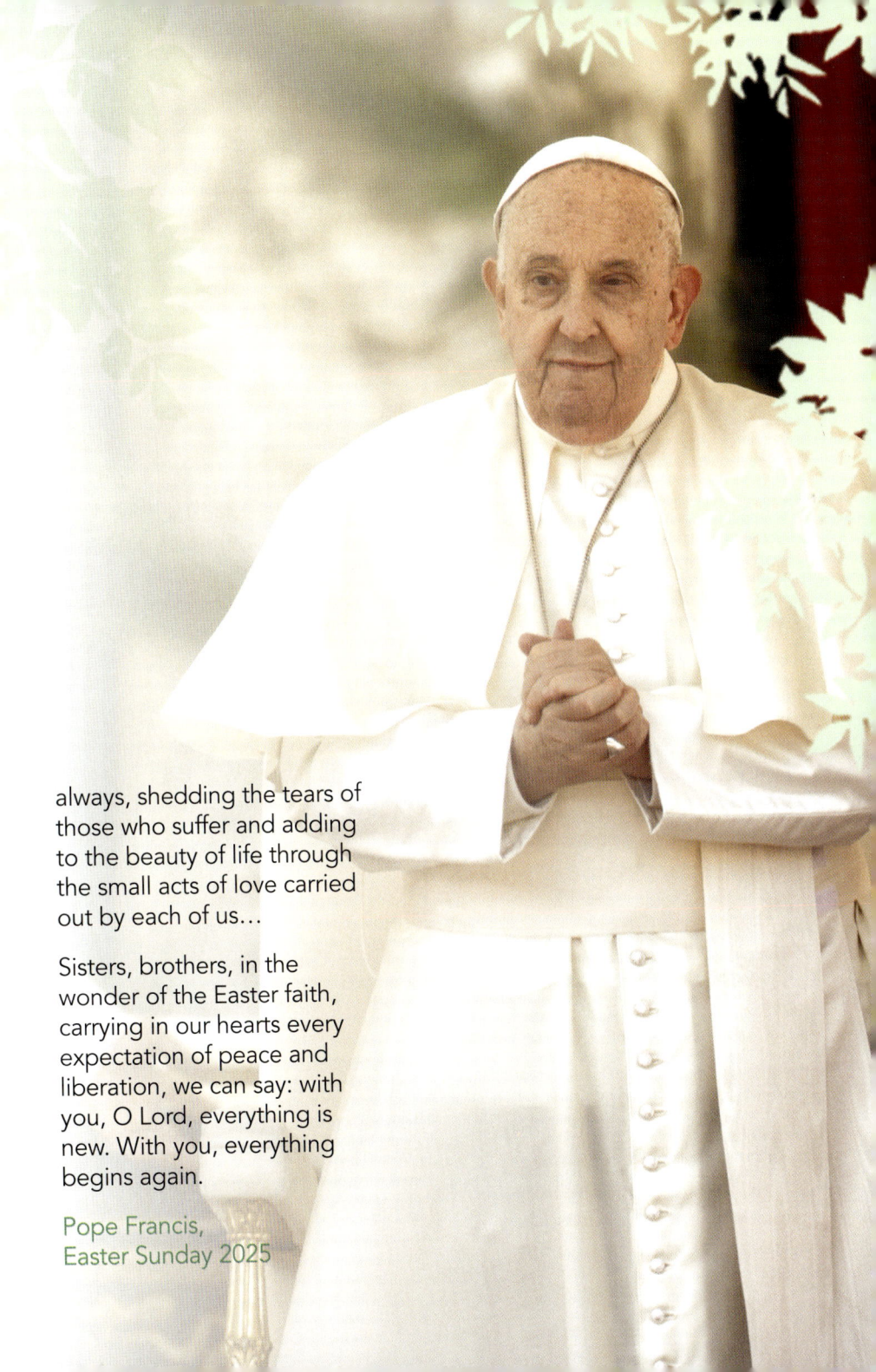

Sisters, brothers, in the wonder of the Easter faith, carrying in our hearts every expectation of peace and liberation, we can say: with you, O Lord, everything is new. With you, everything begins again.

Pope Francis,
Easter Sunday 2025

A NEW VISION OF REALITY

Renowned Franciscan scholar, writer, poet and leader of Franciscan pilgrimages, Fr Murray Bodo OFM sees the parallels between St Francis of Assisi and Pope Francis.

Crossing borders and overcoming barriers, if done with love, also bring a new vision of reality that enables us to have a tender reverence for everything that is. St Francis' followers said that he used to spare lamps, lights, and candles because of the Eternal Light they symbolised. That's a bit over the top, but that is who St Francis was, someone a bit over the top because of what his deep looking had led him to see.

His vision of God radiated from God's creatures, even though he himself, during his last years, was blind because of a disease he contracted in Egypt during the Fifth Crusade. He had gone to Egypt to try to bring peace between Christians and Muslims. The Crusaders laughed at him, but Sultan Malik al-Kamil listened to him, and they became friends, each of them apparently having embraced what he found foreign or even repulsive in the other.

They were open to one another because both had come to value peace over war. Each of them must have done his own inner work. And that is what everyone must do if we are to have peace and effect a revolution of tenderness. We must restructure our own lives, working daily to make ourselves peaceful people.

The image that comes to mind is that of St Francis taming the wolf of Gubbio. He could reach out and calm the wolf; he could bless the wolf because he himself had restructured his own life, going from the desire for knighthood and being caught up in the bloodlust of war, to the man who spoke tenderly to animals and birds, who blessed the violent city of Assisi where he was born and spent his childhood, who worked mercy with lepers and brought reconciliation between the quarrelling mayor and the Bishop of Assisi. These are images of peace-making. Practically every gesture of his life after his conversion was a gesture of peace. And that happened because he was daily becoming a peaceful person. What he says to us today is what he said to his brothers at the end of his life: "I have done what was mine to do; may the Lord show you what is yours to do."

Murray Bodo, OFM, is a poet and award-winning author of many books, including *Francis: the Journey and the Dream*.

LAUDATO SI': POPE FRANCIS' GIFT OF LIFE TO A FAILING WORLD

Mary Colwell found, in Laudato si', that a pope cherished the fur, feathers, petals, soil and woody bark of the natural world.

When rain falls on parched ground the profusion of life that is released can be breathtaking. Seeds that have lain dormant swell and grow into blooms so colourful it is as though an artist has spread a bright palette far and wide. Insects, birds and mammals move into the flower-rich meadow and it becomes vibrant with sight, sound and heady fragrance.

That is how my soul felt when Laudato si' was published in 2015. Pope Francis' words rained down and watered what I knew to be buried truths. For the first time I truly accepted that a pope cherished the fur, feathers, petals, soil and woody bark of the natural world. Here was a man whose heart loved the nature of the planet and he revelled in its innate glory. He cared, not only because nature is useful to us and provides resources for our industry and food for hungry mouths, but also because all creatures have their own dignity that is not dependent on us. There is an abundance of existence outside of humanity that receives God's love, that is worthy simply because it exists.

This conviction he shared with the saint whose name he took when he became Bishop of Rome, Francis. In the beginning of Laudato si' he acknowledges his debt to St Francis and wrote, "His response to the world around him was so much more than intellectual appreciation or economic calculus, for to him each and every creature was a sister united to him by bonds of affection." And it mattered not one jot whether that creature was a bird that dazzled with colour and song or a giant whale that produced awe and wonder; it was irrelevant how small or humble, St Francis knew in his heart that he was connected to other life at the deepest level. When his praise lifted to heaven he was joined by a mighty, natural throng. It is this understanding that infuses Laudato si', making it a work that is as revolutionary as it is rooted in the ancient, beating heart of Catholicism. Just after this encyclical spread around the world a Catholic academic I met said, "For the first time, I knew the pigeons in the streets mattered."

And matter they do, the pigeons, pigs and porpoises of this planet. Francis called them blessed fellow travellers. "In union with all creatures, we journey through this land seeking God." But he went further: he placed creaturely life in heaven. "Eternal life will be a shared experience of awe, in which each creature, resplendently transfigured, will take its rightful place." This was revolutionary, challenging long held ideas, and it was utterly wonderful to read. It made redundant the teaching I had received as child, that only people can enter heaven. For me, a heaven devoid of other life was a poor vision; monochrome and constrained. My young mind could not imagine why God would want to exclude those very things

that make this planet unique and resplendent. On the day the Encyclical was released, beautiful, bright, ferocious wildlife reclaimed its place.

Pope Francis also turned his contemplative gaze to our responsibility for life on earth. Astonishingly, he asked us to become field biologists. In one of the most extraordinary passages he wrote:

"Because all creatures are connected, each must be cherished with love and respect, for all of us as living creatures are dependent on one another. Each area is responsible for the care of this family. This will require undertaking a careful inventory of the species which it hosts, with a view to developing programmes and strategies of protection with particular care for safeguarding species heading towards extinction."

I read and re-read those words, wondering if I had misunderstood their meaning, but it is clear. Our love for God includes a love for the world upon which we dwell and we must become so familiar with it that we can decipher what is in need of protection, and then we must do all we can to save it. To let any species slip away because of our neglect is utterly wrong.

Each year sees the disappearance of thousands of plant and animal species which we will never know, which our children will never see, because they have been lost for ever. The great majority become extinct for reasons related to human activity. Because of us, thousands of species will no longer give glory to God by their very existence, nor convey their message to us. We have no such right.

This is powerful, direct and uncompromising. There is no wriggle-room. We are entrusted with a glorious earth and our many failings are making it threadbare, a poor gift to pass onto the next generation. Under Pope Francis to be a Catholic is to be an environmentalist.

For me, this most wonderful of popes had the head of a Jesuit and the heart of a Franciscan. He truly understood who and what we are and our place on a living, breathing planet. The love he felt for the natural world couldn't help but flow out from his soul and onto the page. He dug deep into the true meaning of Catholicism and found great beauty, but also urgency. As Pope Benedict laid the foundation for action on climate change, Francis embraced the plight of the fellow creatures that dwell alongside. So rapid is the rate of extinction and the destruction of habitats that Francis threw down the gauntlet - be true to your faith and protect the natural world. It is now up to Catholics worldwide to respond and transform the earth.

Laudato si' will forever be Pope Francis' gift of life to a failing world. It is a profound and poetic document. The famed poet, Robert Frost, wrote that, "A poem begins as a lump in the throat, a sense of wrong, a homesickness, a lovesickness." I personally have no doubt that when Pope Francis sat down to write *Laudato si'*, it was just this feeling that compelled him, and the world is surely infinitely better for it.

Mary Colwell, natural history programme producer and writer, counts, among her many awards, the 2022 RSPB Medal for her outstanding contribution to conservation. http://www.curlewmedia.com/

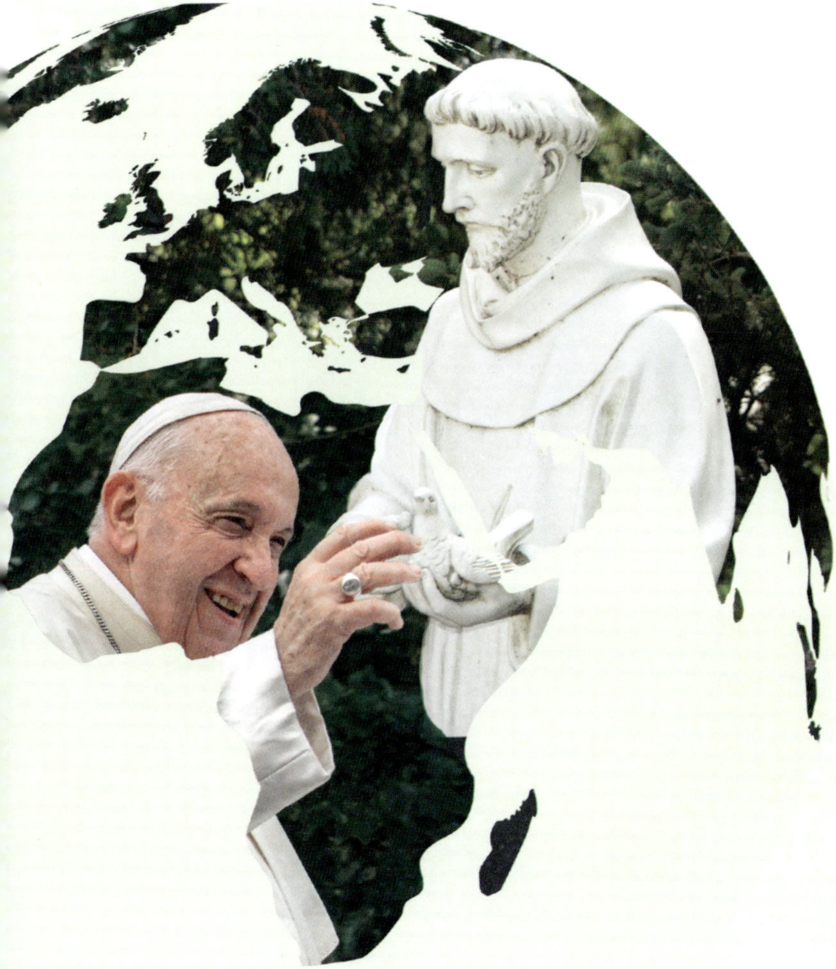

CONTENTS

Foreword by Br Guy Consolmagno SJ
Introduction
1   Praise be to you, my Lord
2   Care for our world
3   Flowers speak of God
4   Preserve natural loveliness
5   Remember the knock-on effect
6   Do I *want* or do I *need*?
7   The richness of water
8   The problem of water
9   Values not for exploitation
10 Protect people
11 Hear the cry of the earth *and* the cry of the poor
12 Money is the root of all evil
13 Think outside the box
14 We were conceived in the heart of God
15 We are called to respect creation
16 Celebrate our creator
17 Appreciate our God-given possibilities
18 All for one and one for all
19 Listen to God speaking in creation
20 Woven together by love
21 Collective goodness
22 God the artist
23 Have power: use it wisely
24 Recover beauty
25 Restore the natural world *and* humanity
26 Attitudes to work affect the environment
27 Work is a vocation
28 Everything is interconnected
29 Safeguard culture
30 Respect quality of life

Added Extras

A Prayer for our Earth
Prayers from a Garden, by Clifford Birchall
Mighty Oaks, by Sr Janet Fearns FMDM
Reach for a Star, by Sr Janet Fearns FMDM
Rewilding the World, by Mary Colwell
I See, by "T"
Keeping on Track, by Cdr Ian Crabtree KSG RN (rtd)
Look at the Stars, by Br Guy Consolmagno SJ

FOREWORD
Br Guy Consolmagno SJ

What is the proper place of humanity in relationship to Creation? Most of us know (even if we do not always behave that way) that Creation is not something we can exploit, willy-nilly, as we please. If nothing else, that doesn't work; abuse Nature too much, and there will not be any Nature left to exploit.

But there is a fascinating counterpoint to this problem that our two champions called Francis raise.

Thinking of what St Francis and Pope Francis have written under the common title of *Laudato Si'* – "May you be Praised" – I am strongly reminded of the writings of a certain English writer whose biography of the Italian St Francis appeared in 1923, and who died in 1936, the year that the Argentinian Pope Francis was born.

G. K. Chesterton, in his famous book *Orthodoxy*, wanders (as he does) over a wide and entertaining range of topics. But at one point he contemplates the difference between Christianity and its pagan counterparts, ancient and modern. He muses, "The essence of all pantheism, evolutionism, and modern cosmic religion is really in this proposition: that Nature is our mother… Nature was a solemn mother to the worshippers of Isis and Cybele. Nature was a solemn mother to Wordsworth or to Emerson…" But he insists that such a vision is not the Christian vision. "The main point of Christianity was this: that Nature is not our mother: Nature is our sister."

We are not called to be in such awe of Creation that we worship it, pagan-like. Instead, Chesterton comments that, "We can be proud of her beauty, since we have the same father; but she has no authority over us; we have to admire, but not to imitate…"

We have the same Father. That is the recurring insight of the poetic vision of St Francis, who constantly refers to the glory and power of sun, moon, fire, storm and stars as "brother" and "sister". And it puts a special poignancy to what it means when, as Pope Francis outlines, we commit the sin of abuse against Nature: it is an abuse against a fellow family member.

All our sins against the environment are ultimately just the same old deadly sins, as ancient as human history, played out on a larger stage. Pope Francis reminds us that abuse of Nature always shows up first and foremost in the suffering of the poor. (And, eventually, we are all poor.) Greed and envy of others lead us to abuse Creation. But the abuse itself is also a sin, not only against the poor who will suffer but against the Creator who is Father to both Nature and us.

To recognise that when we sin against Creation we are sinning against a fellow child of the Creator leads us to see how we can respond to that sin. The solution is not to withdraw entirely from Nature, as if we could somehow hold it pure against our hopeless corruption. Besides being impossible, it also misses the point of why we were created, why we are also a part of this Nature.

After all, what is any sin but merely the corruption of a good act? The answer to lust is not to avoid all sexual love; the answer to gluttony is not to starve ourselves. That kind of Manichaeism destroys the good with the bad, and it fills us with the tempting illusion that we ourselves have the power to make ourselves perfect. Worse, denies the role of God in our salvation. That, too, is sin.

Instead, seeing Nature as our sibling, says Chesterton, "Gives to the typically Christian pleasure in this earth a strange touch of lightness that is almost frivolity… To St Francis, Nature is a sister, and even a younger sister: a little, dancing sister, to be laughed at as well as loved."

Love and laughter. We deal with Creation not out of awe, or fear, but in joy. That is the key to both books of *Laudato Si'*. We would no more exploit Nature than we would exploit our little sister. We would no more be in fear of Nature than we would fear our little sister. Instead, we take joy in Nature as we take joy in our little sister.

Anyone with siblings knows that love comes with conflict, with mistakes, with tears as well as laughter. We cry because we care. But we endure because we are confident of the love that never goes away, and the love of our common Father. In that love we find the echo of the love that created the world.

Seeing Creation with the eyes of joy unites the vision of St Francis and Pope Francis. It is also curious to note that the joy of Chesterton's life, who led him to Christianity and modelled all other loves to him, was his beloved wife… who was also named Frances.

Br Guy Consolmagno SJ is a renowned meteor and planetary scientist, the Director of the Vatican Observatory and President of the Vatican Observatory Foundation. He even has an asteroid named after him! Through his telescope, he daily sees Planet Earth in its context within the Universe.

INTRODUCTION

While suffering intensely from his physical infirmities, [St Francis of Assisi] announced: "I wish to compose a new hymn about the Lord's creatures, of which we make daily use, without which we cannot live, and with which the human race greatly offends its Creator."

Francis of Assisi: Early Documents,
Vol 1, The Saint – page 113

Eight hundred years ago and way ahead of his time, St Francis of Assisi spoke and wrote about the loveliness of the Creation into which we are inserted. Before anybody else campaigned against climate change, environmental and biodiversity protection, he wrote his *Canticle of the Creatures*, describing the sun, moon, stars, water, fire and the entire living world as our brothers and sisters.

Francis pre-dated the language of today's environmental activists. He'd said all that he had to say when he dictated the *Canticle of the Creatures*. The "little poor man of Assisi" taught by intuitive example, not by academic learning. His life was a parable, which we interpret, expand and develop in the light of today's understanding.

Pope Francis uses today's language to challenge us to wake up to the fragile beauty of our planet.

Sometimes his voice falls on deaf ears. Sometimes, as with his Encyclical, *Laudato si'*, his words touch minds and hearts hungry for leadership in the "care of our common home".

This book attempts to offer 30 reflective days based on the insights of two environmental champions, separated only by time.

The structure of each day's reflection is as follows:

- Reflection from Pope Francis' encyclical, *Laudato si'*: on care for our common world
- An image which conveys the theme of the day
- A brief thought inspired by the picture
- A nature poem or extract
- An idea for a DIY recycling project activity – often child-friendly – to inspire a closer relationship with the natural world
- Reflection from or about St Francis of Assisi
- See, judge and act

A book of this size cannot possibly encompass the entirety of *Laudato si'* or the impact of St Francis of Assisi within thirty days. Inspired by their insights and example, we travel with them through our fragile and beautiful world. With their help, we open our eyes, hearts and hands to the loveliness of Creation. With their help, we can also make a difference.

DAY ONE

PRAISE BE TO YOU, MY LORD
Pope Francis

Canticle of the Creatures, 2021, © Franciscan Missionaries of the Divine Motherhood

"*Laudato si', mi' Signore*" – "*Praise be to you, my Lord*". In the words of this beautiful canticle, St Francis of Assisi reminds us that our common home is like a sister with whom we share our life and a beautiful mother who opens her arms to embrace us. "Praise be to you, my Lord, through our Sister, Mother Earth, who sustains and governs us, and who produces various fruit with coloured flowers and herbs".

This sister now cries out to us because of the harm we have inflicted on her by our irresponsible use and abuse of the goods with which God has endowed her. We have come to see ourselves as her lords and masters, entitled to plunder her at will. The violence present in our hearts, wounded by sin, is also reflected in the symptoms of sickness evident in the soil, in the water, in the air and in all forms of life. This is why the earth herself, burdened and laid waste, is among the most abandoned and maltreated of our poor; she "groans in travail" (*Romans* 8:22). We have forgotten that we ourselves are dust of the earth (*c.f.*, *Genesis* 2:7); our very bodies are made up of her elements, we breathe her air and we receive life and refreshment from her waters.

Laudato Si': on care for our common home: 1, 2, 2015, Pope Francis

REFLECTION

St Francis of Assisi looked at Creation and saw God. Pope Francis, a Jesuit, "sees God in all things".

How often do I stop and think about the beauty of the world around me? Do I watch the sunlight dancing on the ripples of a lake, a stream or the sea and find that my heart is also dancing in their loveliness?

Climate change constantly features in the media. Some of the reports relate to things that are happening far away from where I live. I am unlikely to visit the Amazon, the Arctic or Antarctica so I depend on the television in order to gain some understanding of their beautiful fragility.

Yet there are things that I can do now. I can plant butterfly-friendly flowers and shrubs. A "bug hotel" need not take up much space. An old plant pot can provide shelter to small mammals. Why not nail a nesting box to a tree or fasten one to a drainpipe?

Pied Beauty

Glory be to God for dappled things —
For skies of couple-colour as a brinded cow;
For rose-moles all in stipple upon trout that swim;
Fresh-firecoal chestnut-falls; finches' wings;
Landscape plotted and pieced — fold, fallow, and plough;
And áll trádes, their gear and tackle and trim.

All things counter, original, spare, strange;
Whatever is fickle, freckled (who knows how?)
With swift, slow; sweet, sour; adazzle, dim;
He fathers-forth whose beauty is past change:
Praise him.

Gerard Manley Hopkins (1844-89)

St Francis

Most High, all-powerful, good Lord,
yours are the praises, the glory, and the honour, and all blessing.

To you alone, Most High, do they belong,
and no human is worthy to mention your name.

Praised be to you, my Lord, with all your creatures,
especially Sir Brother Sun,
who is the day and through whom you give us light,
And he is beautiful and radiant with great splendour;
and bears a likeness of you, Most High One.

Canticle of the Creatures, 1226, St Francis

DIY recycling activity
a bug hotel

- Stuff an old plant pot or a piece of clay piping with twigs, leaves and moss.
- Place your bug hotel in a cool, shady spot in your garden.
- Enjoy!

See, judge and act

Do I see our planet as "our common home" and "a sister with whom we share our life"?

How can I raise awareness of the importance of caring for our environment?

DAY TWO

CARE FOR OUR WORLD
Pope Francis

St Francis Preaching to the Birds, Giotto, 1297-99, Wikipedia

I believe that St Francis is the example *par excellence* of care for the vulnerable and of an integral ecology lived out joyfully and authentically. He is the patron saint of all who study and work in the area of ecology, and he is also much loved by non-Christians. He was particularly concerned for God's creation and for the poor and outcast. He loved, and was deeply loved for his joy, his generous self-giving, his openheartedness. He was a mystic and a pilgrim who lived in simplicity and in wonderful harmony with God, with others, with nature and with himself. He shows us just how inseparable the bond is between concern for nature, justice for the poor, commitment to society, and interior peace.

[St] Francis helps us to see that an integral ecology calls for openness to categories which transcend the language of mathematics and biology and take us to the heart of what it is to be human. Just as happens when we fall in love with someone, whenever he would gaze at the sun, the moon or the smallest of animals, he burst into song, drawing all other creatures into his praise. He communed with all creation, even preaching to the flowers, inviting them "to praise the Lord, just as if they were endowed with reason". His response to the world around him was so much more than intellectual appreciation or economic calculus, for to him each and every creature was a sister united to him by bonds of affection. That is why he felt called to care for all that exists.

Laudato Si': on care for our common home: 10,11 2015, Pope Francis

REFLECTION

The beauty of our earth is that it's made for all of us to enjoy. We don't need money in order to look out of a window and enjoy a sunrise or sunset. We can feel the sun's warmth on our faces, allow our hands to play in water and the wind to blow through our hair. God uses Creation to touch us through our senses. "The heavens proclaim the wonder of God."

How often have I allowed myself a few minutes to get away from the hustle and bustle of my daily life, to sit quietly, perhaps with a cup of coffee and a biscuit, and simply luxuriate in the loveliness of our world?

The Windhover

I caught this morning morning's minion, kingdom
of daylight's dauphin, dapple-dawn-drawn Falcon, in his riding
Of the rolling level underneath him steady air, and striding
High there, how he rung upon the rein of a wimpling wing
In his ecstasy! then off, off forth on swing,
As a skate's heel sweeps smooth on a bow-bend: the hurl and gliding
Rebuffed the big wind. My heart in hiding
Stirred for a bird, - the achieve of, the mastery of the thing!

Brute beauty and valour and act, oh, air, pride, plume, here
Buckle! AND the fire that breaks from thee then, a billion
Times told lovelier, more dangerous, O my chevalier!

No wonder of it: shèer plòd makes plough down sillion
Shine, and blue-bleak embers, ah my dear,
Fall, gall themselves, and gash gold vermilion.

Gerard Manley Hopkins (1844-89)

St Francis

St Francis… entered the field and he began to preach to the birds that were on the ground. And quickly the birds that were in the trees all came down to him and together remained still while St Francis finished preaching and did not leave until he gave them his blessing. And, according to what Brother Masseo later told Brother James of Massa, as St Francis went among them, touching them with his tunic, not one of them moved. The substance of St Francis's sermon was this: "My sister birds, you owe much to God your Creator and you ought to praise him always and everywhere because he has given you the freedom to fly everywhere, and has given you two and three layers of clothing. He preserved the seed of you all in the Ark of Noah so that your kind would not disappear. And you are also indebted to him for the element of air that he assigned to you. Furthermore you neither sow nor reap, and God feeds you (Luke 12:24) and gives you the rivers and springs for your drink; and he gives you the mountains and valleys as your refuge, the high trees to make your nests; and since you do not know how to spin or sew, he clothes you, you and your little ones. Therefore, your Creator loves you very much, since he gives you so many benefits. So beware, my sisters, of the sin of ingratitude and always strive to praise God."

Francis of Assisi: Early Documents, Vol 3 – pages 593, 594

DIY recycling activity
a nesting box

Find a bird-friendly place where you can put a nesting box for wild birds. It needs to be:

- at least 3m from the ground to protect it from cats
- somewhere quiet
- protected from heavy rain
- out of direct sunlight so that it isn't too hot inside the box

It doesn't need to be in a garden: a hedge, fence or wall can be an ideal location.

A round, 25mm hole in your box will act as an attractive entrance for small garden birds such as blue, coal and marsh tits. Bigger birds such as a nuthatch, a sparrow or a starling need a larger entrance. Robins and wrens prefer an open-fronted box.

Based on RSPB guidelines

See, judge and act

Environmental pollution refers to the injection of harmful substances in the atmosphere. Environmental pollutants are of four types:

(1) Air pollution; (2) Water pollution;
(3) Land pollution; (4) Noise pollution.

What is the greatest source of pollution in my neighbourhood? Is anybody trying to put things right? Can I join them in their efforts to stop the pollution? Do something today to support local birdlife.

DAY THREE

FLOWERS SPEAK OF GOD
Pope Francis

St Francis, San Damiano, Assisi,
© Sr Janet Fearns

St Francis, faithful to Scripture, invites us to see nature as a magnificent book in which God speaks to us and grants us a glimpse of his infinite beauty and goodness. "Through the greatness and the beauty of creatures one comes to know by analogy their maker" (Wisdom 13:5); indeed, "his eternal power and divinity have been made known through his works since the creation of the world" (Romans 1:20). For this reason, Francis asked that part of the friary garden always be left untouched, so that wildflowers and herbs could grow there, and those who saw them could raise their minds to God, the Creator of such beauty. Rather than a problem to be solved, the world is a joyful mystery to be contemplated with gladness and praise.

Laudato Si': on care for our common home: 12, 2015, Pope Francis

REFLECTION

The amazing thing about a wild forget-me-not is that each blue flower has a white, cream or yellow centre. If God can take so much care of a tiny wildflower, how much more care does he take of me!

Easter

The air is like a butterfly
With frail blue wings.
The happy earth looks at the sky
And sings.

Joyce Kilmer (1886-1918)

St Francis

Praised be you, my Lord, through our Sister Mother Earth,
who sustains and governs us,
and who produces various fruit with coloured flowers and herbs.

Canticle of the Creatures, 1226, St Francis

DIY recycling activity
seed bombs (great fun for small children!)

In a bowl, mix:

- One cup of flower seeds (wildflowers or from your garden),
- Five cups of compost,
- 2-3 cups of clay soil.
- Slowly add water until your mixture is sticky enough to be rolled into firm balls.
- Toss the seed bombs into bare parts of your garden.

See, judge and act

Community gardens help to protect our environment. Because people are growing the food that they will eat, the gardens are a form of local, sustainable agriculture with little or no food transportation costs. There is little wastage of water and humans, plants and animals all benefit from the improved ecology of the area.

Could a patch of wasteland near me become a community garden?

What needs to be done?

Identify a corner of my garden – or plant pots on my windowsill – which could be used to grow wildflowers and/or geraniums to attract pollinators.

DAY FOUR

PRESERVE NATURAL LOVELINESS
Pope Francis

Ladywell Lake,
Godalming,
© Sr Janet Fearns

Each year hundreds of millions of tons of waste are generated, much of it non-biodegradable, highly toxic and radioactive, from homes and businesses, from construction and demolition sites, from clinical, electronic and industrial sources. The earth, our home, is beginning to look more and more like an immense pile of filth. In many parts of the planet, the elderly lament that once beautiful landscapes are now covered with rubbish. Industrial waste and chemical products utilised in cities and agricultural areas can lead to bioaccumulation in the organisms of the local population, even when levels of toxins in those places are low. Frequently no measures are taken until after people's health has been irreversibly affected.

These problems are closely linked to a throwaway culture which affects the excluded just as it quickly reduces things to rubbish. To cite one example, most of the paper we produce is thrown away and not recycled. It is hard for us to accept that the way natural ecosystems work is exemplary: plants synthesise nutrients which feed herbivores; these in turn become food for carnivores, which produce significant quantities of organic waste which give rise to new generations of plants.

Laudato Si': on care for our common home: 21, 22, 2015, Pope Francis

REFLECTION

Children in a slum in Paraguay recycled rubbish discarded on a landfill site. They made musical instruments and became known as the Recycled Orchestra.

People in Zambia's shanty towns make spectacular flowers from discarded drink cans.

With sensitivity and insight, loveliness can blossom in the most unexpected places. How much recycling and upcycling happens in my home and workplace? Could I do more?

The Daisy

I know I'm only little.
I know I'm only small,
But I know God loves little ones
The very best of all.

And so, I'm glad I'm little
And very glad I'm small,
'Cos then I know I'm loved by him
Whom I love best of all.

Sr Janet Fearns FMDM

St Francis

Praised be you, my Lord, through Brother Wind,
and through the air, cloudy and serene, and every kind of weather,
through whom you give sustenance to your creatures.

Praised be you, my Lord, through Sister Water,
who is very useful and humble and precious and chaste.

Canticle of the Creatures, 1226, St Francis

DIY recycling activity
a tissue paper flower

- Stack three sheets of tissue paper, cut to 12 x 6 inches (30 x 15 cm), on top of each other.
- Starting with the 6-inch (15 cm) side, fold your paper to make a 1-inch-wide (2.5 cm) concertina.
- Round off the short edges of your concertina with a pair of scissors.
- Loop and twist one end of a green pipe cleaner around the middle of the tissue paper concertina. The pipe cleaner will form the flower stem.
- Gently peel apart the layers of tissue paper – and there's your flower!

See, judge and act

Clean drinking water is essential to life. The human body is made up to sixty per cent water. Because of its importance in many important bodily functions, water needs to be clean and free of disease, metals, and human and animal faeces.

Is there a water source near me which is used as a dumping ground for rubbish?

Can I mobilise people to spend a few hours cleaning out the rubbish?

Will the local Council need to be involved? How?

Clean the gutters and drains around my home of dead leaves.

DAY FIVE

REMEMBER THE KNOCK-ON EFFECT
Pope Francis

Woman carrying a heavy burden, Greccio, © Sr Janet Fearns

Climate change is a global problem with grave implications: environmental, social, economic, political and for the distribution of goods. It represents one of the principal challenges facing humanity in our day. Its worst impact will probably be felt by developing countries in coming decades. Many of the poor live in areas particularly affected by phenomena related to warming, and their means of subsistence are largely dependent on natural reserves and ecosystemic services such as agriculture, fishing and forestry. They have no other financial activities or resources which can enable them to adapt to climate change or to face natural disasters, and their access to social services and protection is very limited. For example, changes in climate, to which animals and plants cannot adapt, lead them to migrate; this in turn affects the livelihood of the poor, who are then forced to leave their homes, with great uncertainty for their future and that of their children. There has been a tragic rise in the number of migrants seeking to flee from the growing poverty caused by environmental degradation. They are not recognized by international conventions as refugees; they bear the loss of the lives they have left behind, without enjoying any legal protection whatsoever. Sadly, there is widespread indifference to such suffering, which is even now taking place throughout our world.

Laudato Si': on care for our common home: 25, 2015, Pope Francis

REFLECTION

A stone tossed into a pond causes ever-expanding ripples. We cannot expect to see the global effects of actions and media on this side of the world. The demand, for instance, for all-the-year-round fresh soft fruit leads to countless acres of polytunnels across former meadows and woodland. An annual migration of seasonal pickers leaves families without a parent for several months – and can also involve trafficking and modern slavery. Damming of rivers for irrigation purposes diminishes the water supply to families and farmers living downstream. Unregulated expansion of farmland has led to vast Amazonian deforestation. You can add many examples from here and abroad.

Sea Fever

I must down to the seas again, to the lonely sea and the sky,
And all I ask is a tall ship and a star to steer her by;
And the wheel's kick and the wind's song and the white sail's shaking,
And a grey mist on the sea's face, and a grey dawn breaking.

I must down to the seas again, for the call of the running tide
Is a wild call and a clear call that may not be denied;
And all I ask is a windy day with the white clouds flying,
And the flung spray and the blown spume, and the seagulls crying.

I must down to the seas again, to the vagrant gypsy life,
To the gull's way and the whale's way where the wind's like a whetted knife;
And all I ask is a merry yarn from a laughing fellow-rover,
And quiet sleep and a sweet dream when the long trick's over.

John Masefield (1878-1967)

St Francis

Blessed is the person who bears with his neighbour in his weakness to the degree that he would wish to be sustained by him if he were in a similar situation (c.f. Galatians 6:2; Matthew 7:12).

Blessed is the servant who loves his brother as much when he is sick and useless as when he is well and can be of service to him. And blessed is he who loves his brother as well when he is far off as when he is by his side, and who would say nothing behind his back he might not, in love, say before his face.

Admonitions XVIII, XXV, St Francis

DIY recycling activity
Unusual plant pots

Children quickly grow out of wellingtons or else manage to damage them so that they become leaky or unwearable whilst remaining colourful and fun. Fill the boots with soil and use them as plant pots. The youngsters will enjoy showing their discarded footwear to their friends!

See, judge and act

When we waste food, we also waste all the energy and water it takes to grow, harvest, transport, and package it. And if food goes to the landfill and rots, it produces methane – a greenhouse gas even more potent than carbon dioxide.

Do I waste food? How can I reduce my food waste? How can I encourage others to reduce their food waste? Does my local Council collect waste food? Do I make my own compost?

Check out and try recipes for "tired" fruit and vegetables.

DAY SIX

DO I *WANT* OR DO I *NEED*?
Pope Francis

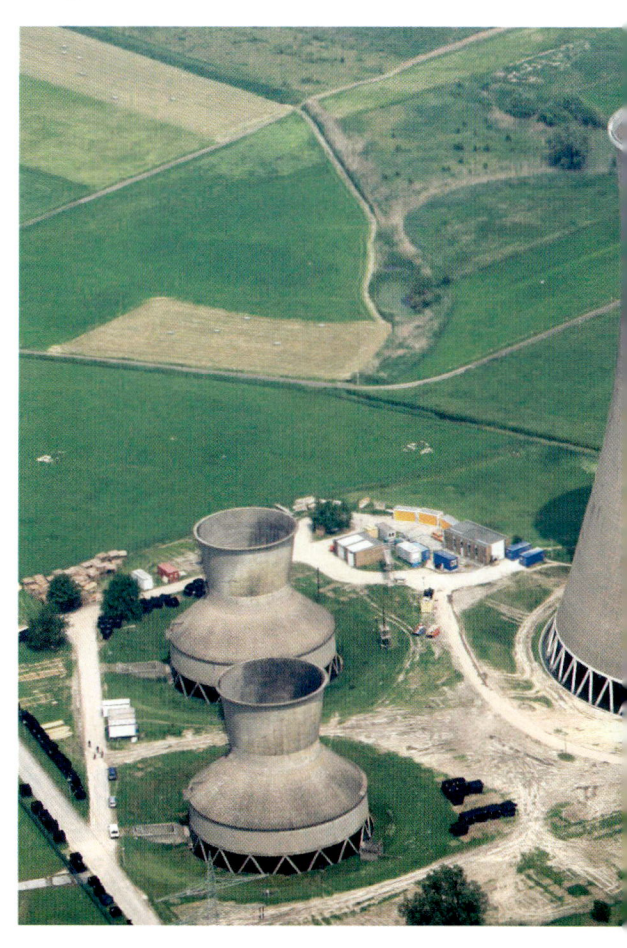

Cooling towers located at power station, Westfalen, Wikimedia

Many of those who possess more resources and economic or political power seem mostly to be concerned with masking the problems or concealing their symptoms, simply making efforts to reduce some of the negative impacts of climate change. However, many

REFLECTION

How often does manufacturing result in goods which we do not need but which successful marketing drives "I want" over "I need"? Do I just *want* or really *need* the latest mobile phone? Why?

Logging in the Amazon is destroying the rainforest at an alarming rate – and for what? The profits from logging benefit the few, not the many.

The Covid-19 lockdown showed us how quickly the natural world can recover if we give it a chance – but are we prepared to offer it the opportunity?

of these symptoms indicate that such effects will continue to worsen if we continue with current models of production and consumption.

Laudato Si': on care for our common home: 26, 2015, Pope Francis

I Watched a Blackbird

I watched a blackbird on a budding sycamore
One Easter Day, when sap was stirring twigs to the core;
I saw his tongue, and crocus-coloured bill
Parting and closing as he turned his trill;
Then he flew down, seized on a stem of hay,
And upped to where his building scheme was under way,
As if so sure a nest was never shaped on spray.

Thomas Hardy (1840-1928)

St Francis

The Apostle says, "the letter kills, but the spirit [brings life]." They are killed by the letter who seek only to know the words that they may be esteemed more learned among others and that they may acquire great riches to leave to their relations and friends.

Admonitions VII, St Francis

DIY recycling activity
a herb garden

- Fix a piece of wood to the bottom of a hanging shoe organiser (to keep it away from the wall).
- Fill each pocket with soil.
- Check that the pockets can drain water: make a couple of holes in the pockets if necessary.
- Plant a few herb seeds in each pocket – or, if you prefer, a few seedlings.
- Hang the organiser on a door, fence or somewhere convenient.
- Keep watered and enjoy!

See, judge and act

Can I grow some of the foods I usually buy?

Is there a local fresh food sharing scheme to which I can contribute some of my surplus fruit and vegetables? If not, what would it take to start such a scheme?

Who could help?

Buy and eat fruit and vegetable mis-shapes which are otherwise perfectly edible.

DAY SEVEN

THE RICHNESS OF WATER
Pope Francis

Somali women collecting water, © Jesuit Refugee Service

Fresh drinking water is an issue of primary importance, since it is indispensable for human life and for supporting terrestrial and aquatic ecosystems. Sources of fresh water are necessary for health care, agriculture and industry. Water supplies used to be relatively constant, but now in many places demand exceeds the sustainable supply, with dramatic consequences in the short and long term… Some countries have areas rich in water while others endure drastic scarcity.

One particularly serious problem is the quality of water available to the poor. Every day, unsafe water results in many deaths and the spread of water-related diseases, including those caused by microorganisms and chemical substances.

Laudato Si': on care for our common home: 28,29 2015, Pope Francis

REFLECTION

In the more developed countries, on the rare occasions that a local water supply is interrupted for some reason, the water company often sends truckloads of bottled water to affected households.

In developing countries, where drinking water is normally collected by the bucketful from a well or stream, women and children walk further and further each day in search of another source. Damming a river or stream to supply nearby farms, industries and towns can cause major problems for people living downstream.

It has often been remarked that the next world war will be fought over the just access to and distribution of, water. The women in the photo are smiling and look happy, but it's tough to collect water, day in and day out, from a communal tap, a lake or a river. The reality is ongoing hard work, for the women and children in the family's unending struggle for survival. Thirst and drought are not pretty.

The Tide in the River

The tide in the river,
The tide in the river,
The tide in the river runs deep.
I saw a shiver
Pass over the river
As the tide turned in its sleep.

                    Eleanor Farjeon (1881-1965)

St Francis

Where there is charity and wisdom,
   there is neither fear nor ignorance.

Where there is patience and humility,
   there is neither anger nor disturbance.

Where there is poverty with joy,
   there is neither covetousness nor avarice.

Where there is inner peace and meditation,
   there is neither anxiousness nor dissipation.

Where there is fear of the Lord to guard the house (c.f. Luke. 11:21),
   there the enemy cannot gain entry.

Where there is mercy and discernment,
   there is neither excess nor hardness of heart.

                                    Admonitions XXVIII, St Francis

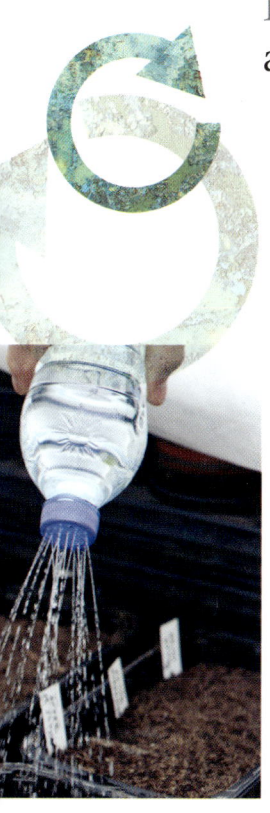

DIY recycling activity
a watering can

- Pierce the lid of a screw-cap bottle with several holes.
- Fill the bottle with water and replace the cap.
- Start watering the plants!

See, judge and act

Water is essential for life and yet huge quantities are wasted or polluted.

How do I waste water?

What can I do to reduce my water usage?

Do I have a water butt or equivalent to collect and use rainwater?

Where could I get one?

Let every member of my household identify a way in which they could each save ten litres of water per day – and stick with it. That's seventy litres per week for each person. It could be a strategy as simple as turning off the tap whilst cleaning teeth.

DAY EIGHT

THE PROBLEM OF WATER
Pope Francis

Access to safe drinkable water is a basic and universal human right, since it is essential to human survival and, as such, is a condition for the exercise of other human rights. Our world has a grave social debt towards the poor who lack access to drinking water, because they are denied the right to a life consistent with their inalienable dignity. This debt can be paid partly by an increase in funding to provide clean water and sanitary

REFLECTION

When life seems to be an endless succession of wet days, puddles and the promise of more rain; when we only need to turn on the tap to have as much water as we need, how many of us think seriously of the difficulties faced by people whose homes do not have a constant water supply – unless, of course, it's in buckets and pots which family members (women and children) have filled at a nearby tap (if they are lucky), well or waterhole?

Think, for a moment, of a true incident in a drought-struck part of Africa. A woman dug a hole in the dried-up riverbed of a seasonal river. The same water which she collected for her family was also where she bathed her children and where her thirsty pigs slaked their thirst. Did she boil the water she took home for drinking? How often did she and her family suffer the effects of drinking polluted water?

Do we take water for granted?

services among the poor. But water continues to be wasted, not only in the developed world but also in developing countries which possess it in abundance. This shows that the problem of water is partly an educational and cultural issue, since there is little awareness of the seriousness of such behaviour within a context of great inequality.

Laudato Si': on care for our common home: 30, 2015, Pope Francis

A Soft Sea Washed around the House

A soft Sea washed around the House
A Sea of Summer Air
And rose and fell the magic Planks
That sailed without a care –
For Captain was the Butterfly
For Helmsman was the Bee
And an entire universe
For the delighted crew.

Emily Dickinson (1830-86)

St Francis

Praised be you my Lord through Sister Water,
So useful, humble, precious and pure.

Praised be you my Lord through Brother Fire,
through whom you light the night and he is beautiful
   and playful and robust and strong.
Praised be you my Lord through our Sister,
Mother Earth
who sustains and governs us,
producing varied fruits with coloured flowers and herbs.

Canticle of the Creatures, 1226, St Francis

DIY recycling activity
leaf mulch

- Collect a pile of leaves and lawn clippings.
- Avoiding hidden twigs, run the lawn mower over your pile to chop up the leaves.
- Mix the chopped-up leaves and grass. (The children will love to help you with this!)
- Spread a thick layer of your mulch around flower beds, trees and shrubs and gardens. The mulch will help to keep down the weeds and, because it also retains moisture, you should be able to do less watering.

See, judge and act

Fertilisers provide crops with nutrients like potassium, phosphorus and nitrogen, which allow crops to grow bigger, faster and to produce more food. Too much fertiliser leads to the release of harmful greenhouse gases into the atmosphere. Fertilisers dissolve in streams and rivers, where they can be toxic to fish and other forms of life once the toxins enter the food chain.

What do I need to do to make my compost more environmentally-friendly?

DAY NINE

VALUES NOT FOR EXPLOITATION
Pope Francis

© Sr Janet Fearns

The earth's resources are also being plundered because of short-sighted approaches to the economy, commerce and production. The loss of forests and woodlands entails the loss of species which may constitute extremely important resources in the future, not only for food but also for curing disease and other uses. Different species contain genes which could be key resources in years ahead for meeting human needs and regulating environmental problems.

It is not enough, however, to think of different species merely as potential "resources" to be exploited, while overlooking the fact that they have value in themselves. Each year sees the disappearance of thousands of plant and animal species which we will never know, which our children will never see, because they have been lost for ever. The great majority become extinct for reasons related to human activity. Because of us, thousands of species will no longer give glory to God by their very existence, nor convey their message to us. We have no such right.

Laudato Si': on care for our common home: 32, 33, 2015, Pope Francis

REFLECTION

The moment when we see the natural world in terms of "resources", we fail to be silenced by loveliness.

If rocks are potential quarries, we ignore the wildlife which makes its home in the cracks and crags, overlook the plants which transform bare rocks into multicoloured mysteries of beauty, become deaf to birdsong, the buzzing of insects and the rustling of leaves.

If we lose the ability to wonder at streams and waterfalls, even the mighty crashing of waves cannot stir our hearts.

Reducing our world to "resources", enriches our pockets at the expense of our souls.

To a Butterfly

I've watched you now a full half-hour,
Self-poised upon that yellow flower;
And, little Butterfly! Indeed
I know not if you sleep or feed.
How motionless! – not frozen seas
More motionless! And then
What joy awaits you, when the breeze
Hath found you out among the trees,
And calls you forth again!

This plot of orchard-ground is ours;
My trees they are, my Sister's flowers.
Here rest your wings when they are weary;
Here lodge as in a sanctuary!
Come often to us, fear no wrong;
Sit near us on the bough!
We'll talk of sunshine and of song,
And summer days when we were young;
Sweet childish days, that were as long
As twenty days are now.

William Wordsworth (1770-1850)

St Francis

Praised be you, my Lord, through Sister Moon and the stars,
in heaven you formed them clear and precious and beautiful.

Canticle of the Creatures, 1226, St Francis

DIY recycling activity
a palace

William, aged 7, built a "guinea pig palace" for his pet, Cinnamon, using five bricks, two carrots and the peel of half a grapefruit.

Could you make a palace for a pet?

Suggested by William's Granny, Sheila Ryding

See, judge and act

Pollination is the act of transferring pollen grains from the male anther of a flower to the female stigma in order to produce fertile seeds. Without pollinators, countless species of plants would die out.

What pollinators do I have in my garden?

Can I identify them individually?

What garden plants are "butterfly-friendly"?

Set up (or extend) a small wildflower patch in my garden.

Organise a community wildflower area, perhaps on some waste ground.

DAY TEN

PROTECT PEOPLE
Pope Francis

Angels Unawares,
Timothy Schmalz

Human beings too are creatures of this world, enjoying a right to life and happiness, and endowed with unique dignity. So we cannot fail to consider the effects on people's lives of environmental deterioration, current models of development and the throwaway culture…

In some places, rural and urban alike, the privatization of certain spaces has restricted people's access to places of particular

REFLECTION

How can we struggle to preserve the environment and yet ignore the often dire needs of the people of this world? Do we treat everyone with the dignity and respect they deserve as children of God? Do we try to strike a balance? Are eco-friendly homes and projects sometimes beyond the reach of people who are asking for food, clothing, shelter, equality and education?

beauty. In others, "ecological" neighbourhoods have been created which are closed to outsiders in order to ensure an artificial tranquillity. Frequently, we find beautiful and carefully manicured green spaces in so-called "safer" areas of cities, but not in the more hidden areas where the disposable of society live.

Laudato Si': on care for our common home: 43,45, 2015, Pope Francis

Stream of Life

The same stream of life that runs through my veins night and day
runs through the world and dances in rhythmic measures.
It is the same life that shoots in joy through the dust of the earth
in numberless blades of grass
and breaks into tumultuous waves of leaves and flowers.
It is the same life that is rocked in the ocean-cradle of birth
and of death, in ebb and in flow.
I feel my limbs are made glorious by the touch of this world of life.
And my pride is from the life-throb of ages dancing in my blood
this moment.

Rabindranath Tagore (1861-1941)

St Francis

Once, as he was sitting in a boat near a harbour on the lake of Rieti, a certain fisherman caught a big fish commonly called a tench and brought it to Francis. He received it joyfully and kindly, took to calling it "brother," and, having placed it in the water next to his boat, began to bless the name of the Lord. For some time, while Francis tended to his prayer, the fish played in the water near the boat, nor did he leave the area until the holy man of God, his prayer completed, gave him permission to go.

The Treatise on the Miracles of Saint Francis (1250-52), Thomas of Celano

DIY recycling activity
a garden pond

- Even a tiny garden can accommodate a small pond which can be a wonderful wildlife habitat. An old washing-up bowl can be put in a hole in the ground and surrounded by pebbles and plants. Placed in a shady spot to reduce evaporation and the water levels regularly monitored, it can be a constant source of interest and delight.

- If you don't have a garden, try making a miniature garden using a kitchen tray, a cereal bowl or equivalent and some gravel or pebbles, perhaps with a small rockery plant or cactus to add some colour. The tray might fit on a veranda or in a corner of a back yard. Keep the bowl topped-up with water (preferably rainwater).

See, judge and act

If possible, visit a local nature reserve and see how they use water to encourage wildlife.

DAY ELEVEN

HEAR THE CRY OF THE EARTH *AND* THE CRY OF THE POOR

Pope Francis

The Stonebreaker 1858, John Brett

The human environment and the natural environment deteriorate together; we cannot adequately combat environmental degradation unless we attend to causes related to human and social degradation. In fact, the deterioration of the environment and of society affects the most vulnerable people on the planet… For example, the depletion of fishing reserves especially hurts small fishing communities without the means to replace those resources; water pollution particularly affects the poor who cannot buy bottled water; and rises in the sea level mainly affect impoverished coastal populations who have nowhere else to go. The impact of present imbalances is also seen in the premature death of many of the poor, in conflicts sparked by the shortage of resources, and in any number of other problems which are insufficiently represented on global agendas.

It needs to be said that, generally speaking, there is little in the way of clear awareness of problems which especially affect the excluded. Yet they are the majority of the planet's population, billions of people. These days, they are mentioned in international political and economic discussions, but one often has the impression that their problems are brought up as an afterthought, a question which gets added almost out of duty or in a tangential way, if not treated merely as collateral damage. Indeed, when all is said and done, they frequently remain at the bottom of the pile. This is due partly to the fact that many professionals, opinion makers, communications media and centres of power, being located in affluent urban areas, are far removed from the poor, with little direct contact with their problems. They live and reason from the comfortable position of a high level of development and a quality of life well beyond the reach of the majority of the world's population. This lack of physical contact and encounter, encouraged at times by the disintegration of our cities, can lead to a numbing of conscience and to tendentious analyses which neglect parts of reality. At times this attitude exists side by side with a "green" rhetoric. Today, however, we have to realise that a true ecological approach always becomes a social approach; it must integrate questions of justice in debates on the environment, so as to hear both the cry of the earth and the cry of the poor.

Laudato Si': on care for our common home: 48,49, 2015, Pope Francis

REFLECTION

The little boy is breaking up flint into smaller stones with his hammer, earning money to keep himself and his unseen family alive. Surrounded by idyllic countryside, the onlooker sees poverty as romantic rather than as hardship. We see nothing of the child's hunger and aching limbs. Was it really a pleasure to spend day after day breaking stones rather than having a chance to enjoy his childhood? How often, today, do we see the end products of people employed at or below a living wage and fail to see the men, women and children who created them?

The Sad Mother

Sleep, sleep, my beloved,
without worry, without fear,
although my soul does not sleep,
although I do not rest.
Sleep, sleep, and in the night
may your whispers be softer
than a leaf of grass,
or the silken fleece of lambs.
May my flesh slumber in you,
my worry, my trembling.
In you, may my eyes close
and my heart sleep.

Gabriela Mistral (1889-1957)

St Francis

When blessed Francis, fleeing, as was his custom, from the sight of human company, came to stay in a certain hermitage, a falcon nesting there bound itself to him in a great covenant of friendship. At night-time with its calling and noise, it anticipated the hour when the saint would usually rise for the divine praises. The holy one of God was very grateful for this because the falcon's great concern for him shook him out of any lazy sleeping-in. But when the saint was burdened more than usual by some illness, the falcon would spare him, and would not announce such early vigils. As if instructed by God, it would ring the bell of its voice with a light touch about dawn.

The Treatise on the Miracles of Saint Francis (1250-52), Thomas of Celano

DIY recycling activity
a woodland den

Children will have a wonderful time creating a den from the dead branches lying around a woodland area – but it's worth remembering that for some creatures, this might be their home. This is an idea for a DIY recycling activity with a social message. When there are natural disasters, fighting or extreme poverty, people use whatever they can find to build shelters. Often they might find enough wood to build the frame of a shelter but then depend on sticks, grass, discarded plastic bags and anything else they can find to keep it waterproof.

See, judge and act

Eighty per cent of plastic water bottles end up in landfills. It takes up to 1,000 years for every single bottle of water to decompose. Each bottle leaks harmful chemicals into our environment as it decomposes.

How much bottled water do I buy and drink?

Buy a reusable water bottle and use tap water, perhaps using a home-made water filter.

DAY TWELVE

MONEY IS THE ROOT OF ALL EV[IL]
Pope Francis

The Misers
© Sr Janet Fearns

Some countries are gradually making significant progress, developing more effective controls and working to combat corruption. People may well have a growing ecological sensitivity, but it has not succeeded in changing their harmful habits of consumption which, rather than decreasing, appear to be growing all the more. A simple example is the increasing use and power of air-conditioning. The markets, which immediately benefit from sales, stimulate ever greater demand. An outsider

REFLECTION

Someone who is obsessed by their bank balance doesn't have time to think of anybody or anything else, do they? Who'd notice the gold of a dandelion in preference to the gold in their pocket?

looking at our world would be amazed at such behaviour, which at times appears self-destructive.

In the meantime, economic powers continue to justify the current global system where priority tends to be given to speculation and the pursuit of financial gain, which fail to take the context into account, let alone the effects on human dignity and the natural environment. Here we see how environmental deterioration and human and ethical degradation are closely linked. Many people will deny doing anything wrong because distractions constantly dull our consciousness of just how limited and finite our world really is. As a result, "Whatever is fragile, like the environment, is defenceless before the interests of a deified market, which become the only rule".

Laudato Si': on care for our common home: 55, 56, 2015, Pope Francis

Love's Lantern

Because the road was steep and long
And through a dark and lonely land,
God set upon my lips a song
And put a lantern in my hand.

Through miles on weary miles of night
That stretch relentless in my way
My lantern burns serene and white,
An unexhausted cup of day.

O golden lights and lights like wine,
How dim your boasted splendours are.
Behold this little lamp of mine;
It is more star-like than a star!

Joyce Kilmer (1886-1918)

St Francis

While he was staying in a poor place the holy man used to drink from a clay cup. After his departure, with wonderful skill bees had constructed the little cells of their honeycomb in it, wonderfully indicating the divine contemplation he drank in at that place.

The Treatise on the Miracles of Saint Francis (1250-52), Thomas of Celano

DIY recycling activity
a planter

We usually throw empty cardboard toilet roll holders in the recycling bin. However, try filling some with soil and planting a seed or two. When the seedling is big enough, simply plant them in a pot or the garden – still in the toilet roll holder. The cardboard will rot and nourish the soil and the seedling's roots will be undisturbed and protected.

See, judge and act

Recycling reduces the need for extracting (mining, quarrying and logging), refining and processing raw materials, all of which create substantial air and water pollution. As recycling saves energy it also reduces greenhouse gas emissions, which helps to tackle climate change.

Does my local council recycle domestic waste? Where is the local recycling facility?

Do I make enough effort to separate my domestic waste into what can be recycled and what goes to landfill?

DAY THIRTEEN

THINK OUTSIDE THE BOX
Pope Francis

The Potato Eaters,
Vincent van Gogh

We can note the rise of a false or superficial ecology which bolsters complacency and a cheerful recklessness. As often occurs in periods of deep crisis which require bold decisions, we are tempted to think that what is happening is not entirely clear. Superficially, apart from a few obvious signs of pollution and deterioration, things do not look that serious, and the planet could continue as it is for some time. Such evasiveness serves as a licence to carrying on with our present lifestyles and models of production and consumption. This is the way human beings contrive to feed their self-destructive vices: trying not to see them, trying not to acknowledge them, delaying the important decisions and pretending that nothing will happen.

Finally, we need to acknowledge that different approaches and lines of thought have emerged regarding this situation and its possible solutions. At one extreme, we find those who doggedly uphold the myth of progress and tell us that ecological problems will solve themselves simply with the application of new technology and without any need for ethical considerations or deep change. At the other extreme are those who view men and women and all their interventions as no more than a threat, jeopardising the global ecosystem, and consequently the presence of human beings on the planet should be reduced and all forms of intervention prohibited. Viable future scenarios will have to be generated between these extremes, since there is no one path to a solution.

Laudato Si': on care for our common home: 59, 60, 2015, Pope Francis

REFLECTION

How do people eat if landowners focus on cash crops and neglect, not only variety, but also the basic staple crops which feed the local population?

We often focus on car production, but what about the supply of bicycles and wheelbarrows to developing countries? Is there a way of boosting local production and distribution?

A single household bicycle and/or a wheelbarrow regularly make the difference between a family's hunger and regular food supply. They both offer employment, education, health care and the transport of goods, food, and agricultural products between the village and the market.

A wheelbarrow or two bikes and a home-made ladder are the local ambulance, transporting a sick person through the bush to the hospital, a journey often taking several hours – or even days. The alternative is to walk, carrying the patient in the arms or on the back – for however long it takes.

Sometimes, what is needed is not new technology but a new tyre or a set of brakes.

"God Pity the Poor!"

"God pity the poor!" I cry.
And I feel a virtuous glow;
Not many so tender as I
To the weight of the sad world's woe.
"God pity the poor!" I shout,
And draw back my garment's hem.
God pities the poor, no doubt;
But how am I pitying them?

Amos Russel Wells (1862-1933)

St Francis

In Greccio a little hare, live and unharmed, was given to St Francis. When it was put down, free to run away where it pleased, at the saint's call it leapt quickly into his lap. The saint gently took it and kindly warned it not to let itself be caught again. He then gave it his blessing and ordered it to return to the woods.

The Treatise on the Miracles of Saint Francis (1250-52), Thomas of Celano

DIY recycling activity
a home to let

You leave out the logs. Small mammals will build their own home.

See, judge and act

Water is too precious to waste. Recycling water means that there is more fresh water available for drinking and cooking.

After washing the dishes, use the water on the garden or use it to flush the toilet.

DAY FOURTEEN

WE WERE CONCEIVED IN THE HEART OF GOD

Pope Francis

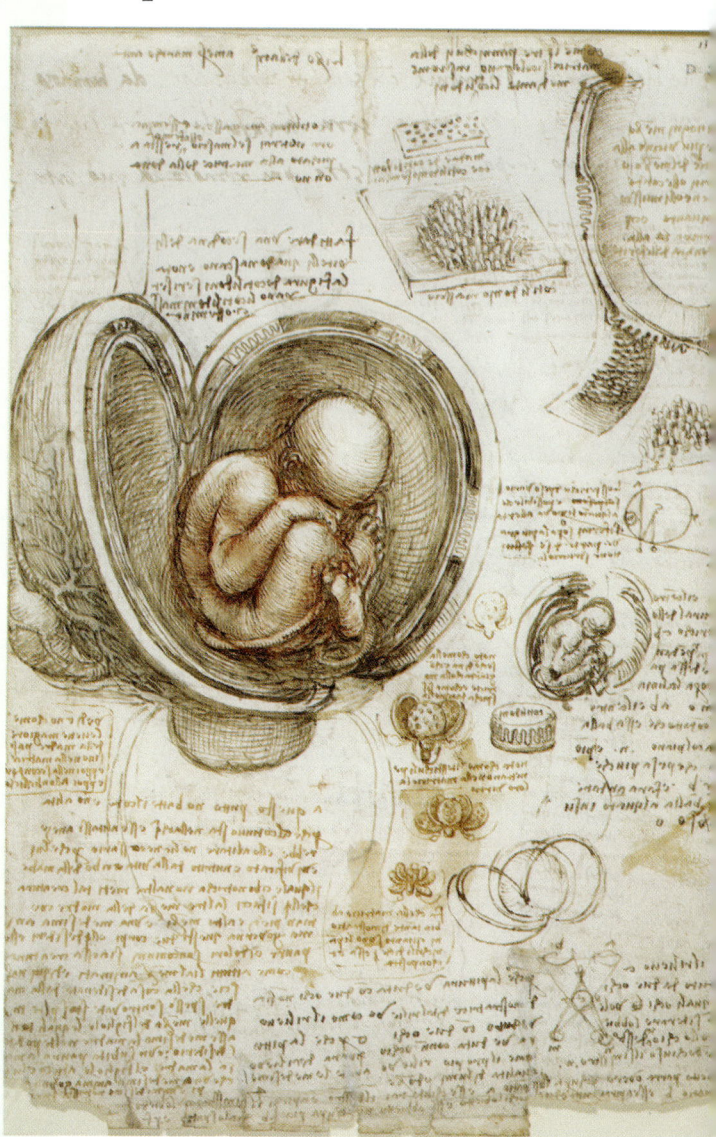

The Foetus in the Womb, 1511, Leonardo da Vinci

The Bible teaches that every man and woman is created out of love and made in God's image and likeness (c.f. Genesis 1:26). This shows us the immense dignity of each person, "Who is not just something, but someone. He is capable of self-knowledge, of self-possession and of freely giving himself and entering into communion with other persons".

St John Paul II stated that the special love of the Creator for each human being "confers upon him or her an infinite dignity". Those who are committed to defending human dignity can find in the Christian faith the deepest reasons for this commitment. How wonderful is the certainty that each human life is not adrift in the midst of hopeless chaos, in a world ruled by pure chance or endlessly recurring cycles! The Creator can say to each one of us: "Before I formed you in the womb, I knew you" (Jeremiah 1:5). We were conceived in the heart of God, and for this reason "Each of us is the result of a thought of God. Each of us is willed, each of us is loved, each of us is necessary."

Laudato Si': on care for our common home: 65, 2015, Pope Francis

REFLECTION

Scientific developments have been phenomenal even in our own lifetime. Our ancestors could never have imagined that the day would come when we could hear the heartbeat of an unborn baby, see it and even perform surgery whilst still in the womb. Yet it only takes a natural event such as an earthquake or a hurricane to highlight our limitations. A starry night can be enough to pray to its Creator, "You are so great, and I am so small".

There are an estimated 7.8 billion people alive on our planet today. Scientists have calculated that there have been "About 105 billion births since the dawn of the human race" with a cut-off date at 50,000 BC – and yet God has known and kept track of every single person. That says something about the immensity of God's love, doesn't it?

Psalm 139

Lord, you have tested me,
  so you know all about me.
You know when I sit down and when I get up.
  You know my thoughts from far away.
You know where I go and where I lie down.
  You know everything I do.
Lord, you know what I want to say,
  even before the words leave my mouth.
You are all around me – in front of me and behind me.
  I feel your hand on my shoulder…

You put me together in my mother's womb.
I praise you because you made me in such a wonderful way.
  I know how amazing that was!

You could see my bones grow as my body took shape,
  hidden in my mother's womb.
You could see my body grow each passing day.
  You listed all my parts, and not one of them was missing.
Your thoughts are beyond my understanding.
  They cannot be measured!
If I could count them, they would be more than all the grains of sand.
  But when I finished, I would have just begun.

Easy-to-Read Version (ERV)

St Francis

Larks are birds that are the friends of light and dread the shadows of dusk. But in the evening when St Francis passed from this world to Christ, when it was already twilight of nightfall, they gathered above the roof of the house, where they circled about noisily for a long while. Whether they were showing their joy or their sadness with their song, we do not know. They sang with tearful joy and joyful tears, either to mourn the orphaned children, or to indicate the father's approach to eternal glory. The city watchmen who were guarding the place with great care were amazed and called others to admire this.

The Treatise on the Miracles of Saint Francis (1250-52), Thomas of Celano

DIY recycling activity
a safe haven

- Don't dump that piece of bark or hollow log. Put it somewhere in the garden as a safe place for small animals to hide from would-be predators.

- Try to identify the songs of three different wild birds. Even if you live in the inner city, you should be able to hear at least three species of wild birds in the area of your home.

- Consider joining a community garden scheme. They exist even in the inner city and allow people to grow and share their vegetables.

- Visit a City Farm.

See, judge and act

Our society has damaged many wildlife habitats.
Set up a bird feeder (or another one) for the local wild birds.
Identify the birds which feed there.

DAY FIFTEEN

WE ARE CALLED TO RESPECT CREATION
Pope Francis

The Indian Ocean from the International Space Station, NASA

We are not God. The earth was here before us and it has been given to us. This allows us to respond to the charge that Judaeo-Christian thinking, on the basis of the Genesis account which grants man "dominion" over the earth (c.f. Genesis 1:28), has encouraged the unbridled exploitation of nature by painting him as domineering and destructive by nature. This is not a correct interpretation of the Bible as understood by the Church. Although it is true that we Christians have at times incorrectly interpreted the scriptures, nowadays we must forcefully reject the notion that our being created in God's image and given dominion over the earth justifies absolute domination over other creatures… "Tilling" refers to cultivating, ploughing or working, while "keeping" means caring, protecting, overseeing and preserving. This implies a relationship of mutual responsibility between human beings and nature. Each community can take from the bounty of the earth whatever it needs for subsistence, but it also has the duty to protect the earth and to ensure its fruitfulness for coming generations…

This responsibility for God's earth means that human beings, endowed with intelligence, must respect the laws of nature and the delicate equilibria existing between the creatures of this world, for "He commanded and they were created; and he established them for ever and ever; he fixed their bounds and he set a law which cannot pass away" (Psalm 148:5b-6). The laws found in the Bible dwell on relationships, not only among individuals but also with other living beings… Together with our obligation to use the earth's goods responsibly, we are called to recognise that other living beings have a value of their own in God's eyes: "By their mere existence they bless him and give him glory," and indeed, "the Lord rejoices in all his works" (Psalm 104:31). By virtue of our unique dignity and our gift of intelligence, we are called to respect creation and its inherent laws, for "the Lord by wisdom founded the earth" (Proverbs 3:19).

Laudato Si': on care for our common home: 67-69, 2015, Pope Francis

REFLECTION

A traditional Zambian proverb points out that from the skies, a village seems peaceful. It is only at close quarters that the difficulties facing a family and a village can be seen. So too, from outer space, planet Earth is spectacularly peaceful and beautiful.

On the ground, we are finding the challenges to the loveliness and natural equilibrium of our world. Satellite imagery, for instance, reveals the smoke from major wildfires where, far below, we see the destruction of human and wildlife habitats, the stress on families and firefighters, and the drastic consequences to ancient forests.

How often do I pray for the members of the emergency services, who risk their lives to save the lives of others? What can I do to make my local environment safer, perhaps by not dropping litter?

God's Grandeur

The world is charged with the grandeur of God.
It will flame out, like shining from shook foil;
It gathers to a greatness, like the ooze of oil
Crushed. Why do men then now not reck his rod?
Generations have trod, have trod, have trod;
And all is seared with trade; bleared, smeared with toil;
And wears man's smudge and shares man's smell: the soil
Is bare now, nor can foot feel, being shod.

And for all this, nature is never spent;
There lives the dearest freshness deep down things;
And though the last lights off the black West went
Oh, morning, at the brown brink eastward, springs—
Because the Holy Ghost over the bent
World broods with warm breast and with ah! bright wings.

Gerard Manley Hopkins (1844-89)

St Francis

Once he went to a village called Alviano to preach. The people gathered and he called for silence. But some swallows nesting there were shrieking so much that he could not be heard at all. In the hearing of all, he spoke to them: "My sister swallows, now it is time for me also to speak, since you have already said enough. Hear the word of God and stay quiet until the word of the Lord is completed." As if capable of reason, they immediately fell silent, and did not leave from the place until the whole sermon was over. All who saw this were filled with amazement and gave glory to God.

The Treatise on the Miracles of Saint Francis (1250-52), Thomas of Celano

DIY recycling activity
a watercress garden

- Pack your half-grapefruit or orange peel with paper towelling or serviettes.
- Scatter watercress seeds on the surface of the water-soaked towel or serviettes.
- Place in a sunny spot – perhaps on your kitchen windowsill – and watch the watercress grow.
- Remember to keep your watercress garden watered!
- When it's ready, enjoy eating your crop!

See, judge and act

Walking improves our quality of life whilst also protecting our natural environment. It helps to reduce air pollution and greenhouse gases.

Walk today instead of using the car, motorbike or public transport.

DAY SIXTEEN

CELEBRATE OUR CREATOR
Pope Francis

The Creation of Adam, 1512, Michelangelo

The psalms frequently exhort us to praise God the Creator, "Who spread out the earth on the waters, for his steadfast love endures for ever" (Psalm 136:6). They also invite other creatures to join us in this praise… We do not only exist by God's mighty power; we also live with him and beside him. This is why we adore him.

A spirituality which forgets God as all-powerful and Creator is not acceptable. That is how we end up worshipping earthly powers, or ourselves usurping the place of God, even to the point of claiming an

REFLECTION

Travel on a bus or train, stand on a station, or just wander through a crowded supermarket or shopping centre and just look at the vast range of faces. No two people have their hair in exactly the same style. Eyes, noses, mouths, skin tones, freckles… they're all different. God can do amazing things with faces, so isn't it just incredible to think about the whole of humanity!

unlimited right to trample his creation underfoot. The best way to restore men and women to their rightful place, putting an end to their claim to absolute dominion over the earth, is to speak once more of the figure of a father who creates and who alone owns the world. Otherwise, human beings will always try to impose their own laws and interests on reality.

Laudato Si': on care for our common home: 67-69, 2015, Pope Francis

Creation

R. *How great is your name, O Lord our God,
through all the earth!*

When I see the heavens, the work of your hands,
the moon and the stars which you arranged,
what is man that you should keep him in mind,
mortal man that you care for him? **R.**

Yet you have made him little less than a god;
with glory and honour you crowned him,
gave him power over the works of your hand,
put all things under his feet. **R.**

All of them, sheep and cattle,
yes, even the savage beasts,
birds of the air, and fish
that make their way through the waters. **R.**

Psalm 8

St Francis

Heading to the hermitage of Greccio, blessed Francis was crossing the lake of Rieti in a small boat. A fisherman offered him a little water-bird so he might rejoice in the Lord over it. The blessed Father received it gladly, and with open hands, gently invited it to fly away freely. But the bird did not want to leave: instead it settled down in his hands as in a nest, and the saint, his eyes lifted up to heaven, remained in prayer. Returning to himself as if after a long stay in another place, he sweetly told the little bird to return to its original freedom. And so the bird, having received permission with a blessing, flew away expressing its joy with the movement of its body.

The Treatise on the Miracles of Saint Francis (1250-52), Thomas of Celano

DIY recycling activity
an egg garden

- When you've eaten the eggs, the box and the eggshells can all be used for planting seeds. There's no need to transplant the seedlings once they germinate: just stick the egg carton, if it's cardboard, in the soil and watch them grow!

- In a book or online, look at the eggs of wild birds that you see near your home. How long do they take to hatch? How many eggs are laid in a clutch? How long do they take to hatch?

See, judge and act

A garden provides homes for birds, insects and other species – and pleasure for people of all ages.

Visit a local park or garden.

DAY SEVENTEEN

APPRECIATE OUR GOD-GIVEN POSSIBILITIES
Pope Francis

The Boat Builders, 1873, Winslow Homer

In this universe, shaped by open and intercommunicating systems, we can discern countless forms of relationship and participation. This leads us to think of the whole as open to God's transcendence, within which it develops. Faith allows us to interpret the meaning and the mysterious beauty of what is unfolding. We are free to apply our intelligence towards things evolving positively, or towards adding new ills, new causes of suffering and real setbacks. This is what makes for the excitement and drama of human history, in which freedom, growth, salvation and love can blossom, or lead towards decadence and mutual destruction. The work of the Church seeks not only to remind everyone of the duty to care for nature, but at the same time "she must above all protect mankind from self-destruction".

Yet God, who wishes to work with us and who counts on our cooperation, can also bring good out of the evil we have done. "The Holy Spirit can be said to possess an infinite creativity, proper to the divine mind, which knows how to loosen the knots of human affairs, including the most complex and inscrutable." Creating a world in need of development, God in some way sought to limit himself in such a way that many of the things we think of as evils, dangers or sources of suffering, are in reality part of the pains of childbirth which he uses to draw us into the act of cooperation with the Creator. God is intimately present to each being, without impinging on the autonomy of his creature, and this gives rise to the rightful autonomy of earthly affairs. His divine presence, which ensures the subsistence and growth of each being, "continues the work of creation". The Spirit of God has filled the universe with possibilities and therefore, from the very heart of things, something new can always emerge: "Nature is nothing other than a certain kind of art, namely God's art, impressed upon things, whereby those things are moved to a determinate end. It is as if a shipbuilder were able to give timbers the wherewithal to move themselves to take the form of a ship."

Laudato Si': on care for our common home: 79, 80, 2015, Pope Francis

REFLECTION

We're all creative in some way or other. The amazing thing is that, the more skilful we become, the longer it can take to create the latest masterpiece and we don't begrudge the time. We become more particular and no longer accept standards which, as a beginner, filled us with pride. Often, looking back at our early efforts is something of an "ouch!" experience and yet we also value those early steps which carried us towards today. With every new creation, we all look towards the moment when we can down tools and step back, knowing that it's as perfect as we can make it.

Doesn't this tell us something about God, the eternal designer and craftsman? St Paul describes us as "God's work of art" (Ephesians 2:13). Until our last breath, God tweaks us and draws us ever closer to perfection. Wow!

Out in the Fields with God

The little cares that fretted me,
I lost them yesterday
Among the fields above the sea,
Among the winds that play,
Among the lowing of the herds,
The rustling of the trees,
Among the singing of the birds,
The humming of the bees.

The fears of what may come to pass,
I cast them all away
Among the clover-scented grass,
Among the new mown hay,
Among the rustling of the corn,
Where drowsy poppies nod,
Where ill thoughts die and good are born,
Out in the fields with God.

Elizabeth Barrett Browning (1806-61)

St Francis

One time as [Francis] was passing through the Spoleto valley, he came upon a place near Bevagna, in which a great multitude of birds of various kinds had assembled. When the holy one of God saw them, because of the outstanding love of the Creator with which he loved all creatures, he ran swiftly to the place. He greeted them in his usual way, as if they shared in reason. As the birds did not take flight, he went to them, going to and fro among them, touching their heads and bodies with his tunic.

Meanwhile his joy and wonder increased as he carefully admonished them to listen to the Word of God: "My brother birds, you should greatly praise your Creator and love him always. He clothed you with feathers and gave you wings for flying. Among all His creatures He made you free and gave you the purity of the air. You neither sow nor reap, He nevertheless governs you without your least care."

At these words, the birds gestured a great deal, in their own way. They stretched their necks, spread their wings, opened their beaks and looked at him. They did not leave the place until, having made the sign of the cross, he blessed them and gave them permission. On returning to the brothers he began to accuse himself of negligence because he had not preached to the birds before. From that day on, he carefully exhorted birds and beasts and even insensible creatures to praise and love the Creator.

The Treatise on the Miracles of Saint Francis (1250-52), Thomas of Celano

DIY recycling activity
flower protector

- It would be lovely to see the orchid growing freely, but it's a tasty morsel for deer, rabbits – and lawnmowers. A few bits of wood and wire netting keep the flower safe, to blossom year after year.

See, judge and act

Wildlife conservation ensures food security. Protecting forests, conserving wildlife and rebuilding forest habitats helps to capture carbon, provides new economic opportunities and guards against erosion, flooding and landslides.

Identify at least five different bird and wildflower species today.

DAY EIGHTEEN

ALL FOR ONE AND ONE FOR ALL
Pope Francis

Creation of Adam in Paradise, Jan Brueghel the Younger

Each of us has his or her own personal identity and is capable of entering into dialogue with others and with God himself. Our capacity to reason, to develop arguments, to be inventive, to interpret reality and to create art, along with other not yet discovered capacities, are signs of a uniqueness which transcends the spheres of physics and biology… The biblical accounts of creation invite us to see each human being as a subject who can never be reduced to the status of an object…

When nature is viewed solely as a source of profit and gain, this has serious consequences for society. This vision of "might is right" has engendered immense inequality, injustice and acts of violence against the majority of humanity, since resources end up in the hands of the first comer or the most powerful: the winner takes all. Completely at odds with this model are the ideals of harmony, justice, fraternity and peace as proposed by Jesus…

The ultimate destiny of the universe is in the fullness of God, which has already been attained by the risen Christ, the measure of the maturity of all things. Here we can add yet another argument for rejecting every tyrannical and irresponsible domination of human beings over other creatures. The ultimate purpose of other creatures is not to be found in us. Rather, all creatures are moving forward with us and through us towards a common point of arrival, which is God, in that transcendent fullness where the risen Christ embraces and illumines all things. Human beings, endowed with intelligence and love, and drawn by the fullness of Christ, are called to lead all creatures back to their Creator.

Laudato Si': on care for our common home: 81-83, 2015, Pope Francis

REFLECTION

In Australia's Barmah Forest, it's easy to see the river red gum trees from which the indigenous communities removed bark for the creation of their everyday tools and equipment. Yet although the bark has been clearly marked out and painstakingly taken down, the tree remains unharmed and flourishes for up to 700 years afterwards. What a contrast to the vast destruction of forests, sometimes over millennia, often for vanity projects, in other parts of the world!

Sometimes people themselves are victims, in addition to the natural resources they try to save. Sr Dorothy Stang SND was murdered in 2005 as a result of her efforts to protect both the Amazon rainforest and its indigenous, impoverished peoples from the greed of illegal loggers. Fr Stan Swamy SJ died in judicial custody in 2021, aged 84, after a lifetime of defending India's Adivasi minorities against a political system which actively discriminated against them.

How long will it be before our planet once again experiences its original harmony between humanity and "the rest"?

All Things Bright and Beautiful

R. *All things bright and beautiful,
all creatures great and small,
all things wise and wonderful,
the Lord God made them all.*

Each little flow'r that opens,
each little bird that sings,
God made their glowing colours,
God made their tiny wings. R.

The purple-headed mountain,
the river running by,
the sunset, and the morning
that brightens up the sky; R.

The cold wind in the winter,
the pleasant summer sun,
the ripe fruits in the garden,
God made them, ev'ry one. R.

God gave us eyes to see them,
and lips that we might tell
how great is God Almighty,
who has made all things well. R.

Cecil Frances Alexander (1818-95)

St Francis

A cricket lived in a fig tree by the cell of the holy one of God at the Portiuncula, and it would sing frequently with its usual sweetness. Once the blessed father stretched out his hand to it and gently called it to him: "My Sister Cricket, come to me!" And the cricket, as if it had reason, immediately climbed onto his hand. He said to it: "Sing, my sister cricket, and with joyful song praise the Lord your Creator!" The cricket, obeying without delay, began to chirp, and did not stop singing until the man of God, mixing his own songs with its praise, told it to return to its usual place. There it remained constantly for eight days, as if tied to the spot. Whenever the saint would come down from the cell he would always touch it with his hands and command it to sing, and it was always eager to obey his commands. And the saint said to his companions: "Let us give permission to our sister cricket to leave, who has up to now made us so happy with her praises, so that our flesh may not boast vainly in any way." And as soon as it had received permission, the cricket went away and never appeared there again. On seeing all this, the brothers were quite amazed.

The Treatise on the Miracles of Saint Francis (1250-52), Thomas of Celano

DIY recycling activity
a minibeast hotel

- Use bricks and pallets to make a solid structure
- Fill with natural materials such as strips of wood, straw, moss, dry leaves, woodchips, old terracotta pots, old roofing tiles, etc.
- Find out the names of three endangered wildlife species in this country. Why are they at risk?

See, judge and act

When plastic is exposed to sunlight, it produces methane and ethylene, which have a detrimental effect. It has been determined that greenhouse gas emissions from the plastic lifecycle account for 3.8 per cent of global greenhouse gas emissions.

Let each member of the household use one less single-use plastic item today.

DAY NINETEEN

LISTEN TO GOD SPEAKING IN CREATION

Pope Francis

Stour Valley and Dedham Church, 1815, John Constable

Our insistence that each human being is an image of God should not make us overlook the fact that each creature has its own purpose. None is superfluous. The entire material universe speaks of God's love, his boundless affection for us. Soil, water, mountains: everything is, as it were, a caress of God. The history of our friendship with God is always linked to particular places which take on an intensely personal meaning; we all remember places and revisiting those memories does us much good. Anyone who has grown up in the hills or used to sit by the spring to drink or played outdoors in the neighbourhood square; going back to these places is a chance to recover something of their true selves.

God has written a precious book, "whose letters are the multitude of created things present in the universe" … This contemplation of creation allows us to discover in each thing a teaching which God wishes to hand on to us, since "for the believer, to contemplate creation is to hear a message, to listen to a paradoxical and silent voice". We can say that "alongside revelation properly so-called, contained in sacred scripture, there is a divine manifestation in the blaze of the sun and the fall of night". Paying attention to this manifestation, we learn to see ourselves in relation to all other creatures: "I express myself in expressing the world; in my effort to decipher the sacredness of the world, I explore my own".

Laudato Si': on care for our common home: 84, 85, 2015, Pope Francis

REFLECTION

There are some artists whose work is a delight to behold. There is always something else to notice, a small detail which, somehow, was previously unseen.

John Constable is one such artist. His superb attention to detail means that no landscape is "just" a countryside scene. One can imagine that he sat for hours, gazing at a potential subject, drinking in the loveliness of every leaf, every blade of grass, every tree, cottage, farm worker…

It's difficult to make time and space for silent contemplation of our natural world and not see God in its diversity and hear God speak in the birdsong and the quiet buzz of insects.

What are some of the lessons I've learned through allowing God to speak to me through Creation?

Spellbound

The night is darkening round me,
The wild winds coldly blow;
But a tyrant spell has bound me
And I cannot, cannot go.
The giant trees are bending
Their bare boughs weighed with snow.
And the storm is fast descending,
And yet I cannot go.
Clouds beyond clouds above me,
Wastes beyond wastes below;
But nothing drear can move me;
I will not, cannot go.

Emily Bronte (1818-48)

St Francis

Once when the man of God was on a journey from Siena to the valley of Spoleto he passed a field where a sizeable flock of sheep were grazing. He greeted them kindly as he usually did, and they all ran to him, raised their heads and returned his friendly greeting with loud bleating. His vicar took careful note of what the sheep had done and, following at a slower pace with the other companions, said to the rest, "Did you see what these sheep did for the holy father? He is truly great whom the dumb animals revere as their father, and those lacking reason recognise as a friend of their Creator."

The Treatise on the Miracles of Saint Francis (1250-52), Thomas of Celano

DIY recycling activity
Recycle your thoughts

If possible, sit quietly outdoors with a notepad and pencil. Make a list of the sounds that you can hear. Which sounds are natural and which come from cars, trains etc. Focus on the natural sounds and relax in them. Take time to pray.

See, judge and act

The amount of clothing dumped on a landfill site is neither regulated nor controlled. As the fabrics degrade, they release greenhouse gases and speed up climate change. Recycling unwanted clothing slows down the rate of climate change.

Let each member of the household pick out an unused, wearable item of clothing and donate it to the local charity shop.

DAY TWENTY

WOVEN TOGETHER BY LOVE
Pope Francis

Weaver, 1884, Vincent van Gogh

At times we see an obsession with denying any pre-eminence to the human person; more zeal is shown in protecting other species than in defending the dignity which all human beings share in equal measure. Certainly, we should be concerned lest other living beings be treated irresponsibly. But we should be particularly indignant at the enormous inequalities in our midst, whereby we continue to tolerate some considering themselves more worthy than others. We fail to see that some are mired in desperate and degrading poverty, with no way out, while others have not the faintest idea of what to do with their possessions, vainly showing off their supposed superiority and leaving behind them so much waste which, if it were the case everywhere, would destroy the planet…

A sense of deep communion with the rest of nature cannot be real if our hearts lack tenderness, compassion and concern for our fellow human beings. It is clearly inconsistent to combat trafficking in endangered species while remaining completely indifferent to human trafficking, unconcerned about the poor, or undertaking to destroy another human being deemed unwanted. This compromises the very meaning of our struggle for the sake of the environment... Concern for the environment thus needs to be joined to a sincere love for our fellow human beings and an unwavering commitment to resolving the problems of society...

Our indifference or cruelty towards fellow creatures of this world sooner or later affects the treatment we mete out to other human beings. We have only one heart, and the same wretchedness which leads us to mistreat an animal will not be long in showing itself in our relationships with other people. Every act of cruelty towards any creature is "contrary to human dignity"... Everything is related, and we human beings are united as brothers and sisters on a wonderful pilgrimage, woven together by the love God has for each of his creatures and which also unites us in fond affection with brother sun, sister moon, brother river and mother earth.

Laudato Si': on care for our common home: 90-92, 2015, Pope Francis

REFLECTION

When, during the Industrial Revolution, weaving on an industrial scale became possible, many families lost their traditional skills and markets, and faced poverty. Suddenly, those people who had spun wool and woven household goods within their own homes found themselves without an income unless they abandoned their homes and families and moved to the dire conditions of the mills and other factories.

Parliament eventually legislated for a child's working day to be limited to ten hours. Mass industrialisation brought vast profits for some at the cost of mass hunger, family break-up, homelessness, health hazards, illiteracy and cruelty for others. At the same time, the increasingly polluted environment damaged water sources, farmland, air quality, flora and fauna... yet these are realities today for many people in developing countries.

It's hard to believe, isn't it, that oysters, so often the modern delicacy of the affluent, were once the food of the poor, even in Britain?

Poverty and Riches

Who with a little cannot be content,
Endures an everlasting punishment.

Robert Herrick (1591-1674)

St Francis

A nobleman from the area of Siena sent a pheasant to blessed Francis while he was sick. He received it gladly, not with the desire to eat it, but because it was his custom to rejoice in such creatures out of love for their Creator. He said to the pheasant: "Praised be our Creator, Brother Pheasant!" And to the brothers he said: "Let's make a test now to see if Brother Pheasant wants to remain with us, or if he'd rather return to his usual places, which are more fit for him." At the saint's command a brother carried the pheasant away and put him down in a vineyard far away. Immediately the pheasant returned at a brisk pace to the father's cell.

The saint ordered it to be carried out again, and even further away, but with great
stubbornness it returned to the door of the cell, and as if forcing its way, it entered under the tunics of the brothers who were in the doorway. And so the saint commanded that it should be lovingly cared for, caressing and stroking it with gentle words.

A doctor who was very devoted to the holy one of God saw this, and asked the brothers to give it to him, not because he wanted to eat it, but wanting rather to care for it out of reverence for the saint.

What else? The doctor took it home with him, but when separated from the saint it seemed hurt, and while away from his presence it absolutely refused to eat. The doctor was amazed, and at once carried the pheasant back to the saint, telling him in order all that happened. As soon as it was placed on the ground, and saw its father, it threw off its sadness and began to eat with joy.

The Treatise on the Miracles of Saint Francis (1250-52), Thomas of Celano

DIY recycling activity
Peanut bird feeder

(Ideal activity for children on a rainy day!)

Thread a piece of strong cotton through as many unshelled peanuts as you like and then hang them up where the small birds can feast on them. Watch out for squirrels so hang up the peanuts somewhere the squirrels can't also enjoy a free meal!

Idea suggested by Mary Gallagher

See, judge and act

Not mowing the lawn saves fuel and money whilst also helping to rewild our environment.

Don't cut your grass. Go for a walk instead and allow birds and pollinators to enjoy the garden.

If you don't have a garden, go for a walk and enjoy seeing someone else's.

DAY TWENTY-ONE

COLLECTIVE GOODNESS
Pope Francis

Food distribution, Democratic Republic of Congo, © Jesuit Refugee Service

The natural environment is a collective good, the patrimony of all humanity and the responsibility of everyone. If we make something our own, it is only to administer it for the good of all. If we do not, we burden our consciences with the weight of having denied the existence of others. That is why the New Zealand bishops asked what the commandment "Thou shall not kill" means when "Twenty per cent of the world's population consumes resources at a rate that robs the poor nations and future generations of what they need to survive".

Laudato Si': on care for our common home: 95, 2015, Pope Francis

REFLECTION

The frightening thing about hunger – real hunger – is its silence. Even babies and children no longer have the strength to cry. Adults don't have the strength to search for the food that they know is not available. They would complain but it takes energy that isn't theirs – so they sit and wait – and sometimes the waiting is terminal.

When food comes, there is a fight for every grain of rice, provided there is still the capacity for struggle. Otherwise, someone waits until someone else thinks to bring even a mouthful of food. If that lifegiving morsel doesn't come, the hunger and the silent waiting continue…

When were you hungry – really hungry?

Holy Thursday: is this a holy thing to see

Is this a holy thing to see,
In a rich and fruitful land,
Babes reduced to misery,
Fed with cold and usurous hand?

Is that trembling cry a song?
Can it be a song of joy?
And so many children poor?
It is a land of poverty!

And their sun does never shine.
And their fields are bleak & bare.
And their ways are fill'd with thorns.
It is eternal winter there.

For where'er the sun does shine,
And where'er the rain does fall:
Babe can never hunger there,
Nor poverty the mind appal.

William Blake (1757-1827)

St Francis

A certain young man having caught one day a great number of doves, as he was to sell them he met St Francis, who always felt a great compassion for such gentle animals; and, looking at the doves with eyes of pity, he said to the young man: "O good man, I entreat thee to give me those harmless birds, emblems in Scripture of humble, pure, and faithful souls, so that they may not fall into cruel hands, which would put them to death." And the young man, inspired by God, immediately gave them to St Francis, who, placing them in his bosom, addressed them thus sweetly: "O my little sisters the doves, so simple, so innocent, and so chaste, why did you allow yourselves to be caught? I will save you from death, and make your nests, that you may increase and multiply, according to the command of God."

Then St Francis made nests for them all, and they began to lay their eggs and hatch them in presence of the brethren, and were as familiar and as tame with St Francis and the friars as if they had been hens brought up amongst them, nor did they ever go away until St Francis had given them his blessing.

Little Flowers of St Francis, XXII, fourteenth century

DIY recycling activity
an easy bird feeder

- Fasten some string through an empty coconut shell. Pack it with fat and seeds and hang it where small birds can enjoy it.
- Another child-friendly activity: pack a pine cone with fat, seeds or meal worms and hang it where small birds will have a free meal.

Ideas suggested by Mary Gallagher

See, judge and act

Wet wipes, if not properly disposed of, block our drains and sewers, find their way into oceans and cause long-term problems for sea creatures and the marine environment.

Where possible and practical, instead of using antibacterial hand wipes, use soap and water.

DAY TWENTY-TWO

GOD THE ARTIST
Pope Francis

Traditional embroiderer, Seville, Spain, © Sr Janet Fearns

Jesus lived in full harmony with creation, and others were amazed: "What sort of man is this, that even the winds and the sea obey him?" (Matthew 8:27). His appearance was not that of an ascetic set apart from the world, nor of an enemy to the pleasant things of life. Of himself he said: "The Son of Man came eating and drinking and they say, 'Look, a glutton and a drunkard!'" (Matthew 11:19). He was far removed from philosophies which despised the body, matter and the things of the world... Jesus worked with his hands, in daily contact with the matter created by God, to which he gave form by his craftsmanship. It is striking that most of his life was dedicated to this task in a simple life which awakened no admiration at all: "Is not this the carpenter, the son of Mary?" (Mark 6:3). In this way he sanctified human labour and endowed it with a special significance for our development…

In the Christian understanding of the world, the destiny of all creation is bound up with the mystery of Christ, present from the beginning… One Person of the Trinity entered into the created cosmos, throwing in his lot with it, even to the cross. From the beginning of the world, but particularly through the incarnation, the mystery of Christ is at work in a hidden manner in the natural world as a whole, without thereby impinging on its autonomy.

Laudato Si': on care for our common home: 98, 99, 2015, Pope Francis

REFLECTION

Just think of the patience of God! The embroiderer in this photo and two others, working eight hours per day, five days per week, will take three years to create the cloak to be worn by a statue of Our Lady in Seville's annual processions for Holy Week. Yet God created the universe and everything in it! Not only that, God didn't direct the choices of humanity for good or ill, but allowed us to make our own choices, even when they impacted negatively on our beautiful, fragile planet.

Today, as we experience the effects of climate change, time is wasted in arguments for and against doing what is necessary to restore balance. If the embroiderers argued about who would work on which areas of the cloak, it would never be finished – so why do we quarrel about the much bigger project of preservation and conservation?

God the Artist

God, when you thought of a pine tree,
How did you think of a star?
How did you dream of the Milky Way
To guide us from afar.
How did you think of a clean brown pool
Where flecks of shadows are?
God, when you thought of a cobweb,
How did you think of dew?
How did you know a spider's house
Had shingles bright and new?
How did you know the human folk
Would love them like they do?

God, when you patterned a bird song,
Flung on a silver string,
How did you know the ecstasy
That crystal call would bring?
How did you think of a bubbling throat
And a darling speckled wing?

God, when you chiselled a raindrop,
How did you think of a stem,
Bearing a lovely satin leaf
To hold the tiny gem?
How did you know a million drops
Would deck the morning's hem?

Why did you mate the moonlit night
With the honeysuckle vines?
How did you know Madeira bloom
Distilled ecstatic wines?

How did you weave the velvet disk
Where tangled perfumes are?
God, when you thought of a pine tree,
How did you think of a star?

Angela Morgan (1875-1957)

St Francis

In Greccio a little hare, live and unharmed, was given to St Francis. When it was put down, free to run away where it pleased, at the saint's call it leapt quickly into his lap. The saint gently took it and kindly warned it not to let itself be caught again. He then gave it his blessing and ordered it to return to the woods.

The Treatise on the Miracles of St Francis (1250-52), Thomas of Celano

DIY recycling activity
Target!

- Tear up an old newspaper and roll up the pages to make small balls.
- Use a paper bin as your target and see how many of your paper balls you can throw into it from a distance.
- Make it a competition with other family members.
- When you have finished your game, use the paper to make mulch for your garden.

See, judge and act

Mulch reduces soil water loss and erosion whilst improving soil aeration and drainage.

Dampen and use the contents of your paper shredder as a mulch for your garden or planters. Shredded paper is apparently wonderful for cabbage growers!

DAY TWENTY-THREE

HAVE POWER: USE IT WISELY
Pope Francis

Humanity has entered a new era in which our technical prowess has brought us to a crossroads. We are the beneficiaries of two centuries of enormous waves of change: steam engines, railways, the telegraph, electricity, automobiles, aeroplanes, chemical industries, modern medicine, information technology and, more recently, the digital revolution, robotics, biotechnologies and nanotechnologies. It is right to rejoice in these advances and to be excited by the immense possibilities which they continue to open up before us, for "science and technology are wonderful products of a God-given human creativity"...

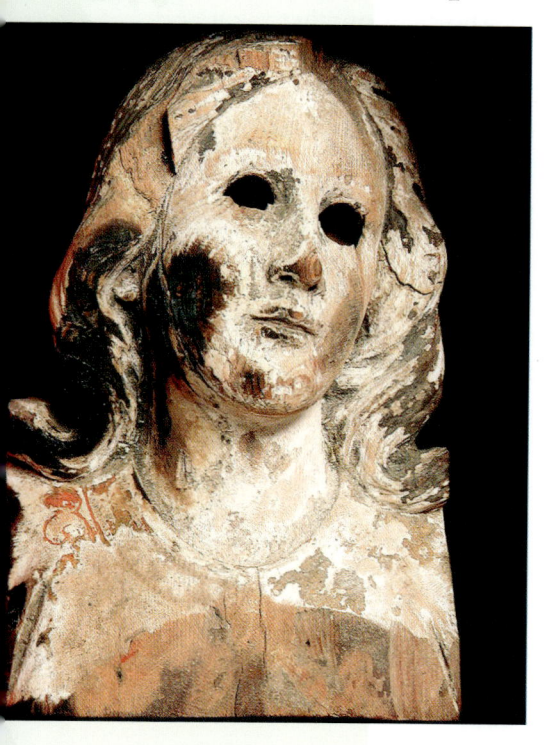

Our Lady of Nagasaki
(Unknown artist)

Technoscience, when well directed, can produce important means of improving the quality of human life, from useful domestic appliances to great transportation systems, bridges, buildings and public spaces. It can also produce art and enable men and women immersed in the material world to "leap" into the world of beauty...

Yet it must also be recognised that nuclear energy, biotechnology, information technology, knowledge of our DNA, and many other abilities which we have acquired, have given us tremendous power. More precisely, they have given those with the knowledge, and especially the economic resources to use them, an impressive dominance over the whole of humanity and the entire world. Never has humanity had such power over itself, yet nothing ensures that it will be used wisely, particularly when we consider how it is currently being used…

There is a tendency to believe that every increase in power means "an increase of 'progress' itself…an assimilation of new values into the stream of culture", as if reality, goodness and truth automatically flow from technological and economic power as such. The fact is that "contemporary man has not been trained to use power well", because our immense technological development has not been accompanied by a development in human responsibility, values and conscience… In this sense, we stand naked and exposed in the face of our ever-increasing power, lacking the wherewithal to control it.

Laudato Si': on care for our common home:102-105, 2015, Pope Francis

REFLECTION

What follows is an excerpt from Fr Kaemon Noguchi's letter describing how he discovered Our Lady of Nagasaki in the cathedral ruins

I grew up in Urakami, Ishigami town (Yamanaka) and joined the Hokkaido Trappist Monastery in the fourth year of the Showa era (1929) and was ordained priest in the fourteenth year (1939). I must have been twelve or thirteen years of age when the statue of Virgin Mary arrived from Italy and was placed near the ceiling over the altar of the Urakami Cathedral. Her celestial beauty left a deep impression to my boyhood. I was then irresistibly attracted by the Madonna.

When I was to join the monastery in Hokkaido, I knelt down in front of the altar and prayed to bid my farewell… "Dear Our Lady, I am going far north to the Trappist Monastery in Hokkaido, so this may be the last prayer I offer to you in this cathedral. But wherever I will be, may your protection and guidance be with me as ever." This memory never leaves me after all these years.

In April of the eighteenth year of the Showa era (1943), I was called to arms and returned home in Nagasaki. I enlisted in the Kurume Regiment and was once discharged in January of the twentieth year of the Showa era (1945)…

The war was over on the fifteenth day of August. I was sent home after being discharged in October. Before going back to Hokkaido, I wished to find a keepsake of the cathedral to bring with me. So I went to the ruins of the church and yet I found nothing but a heap of rubble. I searched about the destroyed altar and confessionals of Father Nishida and Father Tamaya for over one hour in vain. I tumbled onto a stone and prayed to Virgin Mary just like when I departed for the monastery as a boy.

I was meant to return to Hokkaido soon. Praying for her guidance, I desperately looked for any broken pieces of liturgics which survived the bombing. Sadly, there was no sign of the cross or the holy statue of the Madonna. I prayed once again to Holy Mother to let me encounter anything at all associated to the church.

Some time passed… I was praying silently. And all of a sudden, I saw the holy face of the Virgin blackened by fire, looking at me with a sorrowful air. I cried with joy. "Thank you, Our Lady. Thank you!"

The destroyed torso might have been buried somewhere but I was too excited holding her head tightly in my arms to think about anything else. What a joy! It is inexplicable how I thanked the Holy Mother. I was half in a dream walking to the house embracing the head…

When Bishop Urakawa visited Trappist, I showed him the head of Madonna and explained to him how I had found it. "You have found the finest treasure indeed. If you had not discovered it, the Madonna would have got lost and most probably would have been disposed of like a piece of rubbish," he said.

Kaemon Noguchi
Hokkaido Trappist Monastery

Music

Sweet melody amidst the moving spheres
Breaks forth, a solemn and entrancing sound,
A harmony whereof the earth's green hills
Give but the faintest echo; yet is there
A music everywhere, and concert sweet!
All birds which sing amidst the forest deep
Till the flowers listen with unfolded bells;
All winds that murmur over summer grass,
Or curl the waves upon the pebbly shore;
Chiefly all earnest human voices rais'd
In charity and for the cause of truth,
Mingle together in one sacred chord,
And float, a grateful incense, up to God.

Bessie Rayner Parkes (1829-1925)

St Francis

He overflowed with the spirit of charity, pitying not only men who were suffering need, but even the dumb brutes, reptiles, birds, and other creatures with and without sensation. But among all kinds of animals he loved little lambs with a special love, and a readier affection, because the humility of our Lord Jesus Christ is, in holy scripture, most frequently and aptly illustrated by the simile of a lamb. So too especially he would embrace more fondly and behold more gladly all those things wherein might be found some allegorical similitude of the Son of God. Thus, when he was once journeying through the March of Ancona, and after preaching God's word in that city had set out towards Osimo... he found in the fields a shepherd feeding a herd of she-goats and he-goats. Among the multitude of goats there was one little sheep, going along in humble fashion and quietly grazing. When Francis saw her he stopped, and, moved in his heart with grief said to the brother who accompanied him, groaning aloud, "Do you not see this sheep, which is walking so meekly among these she-goats and he-goats? I tell you that even so our Lord Jesus Christ walked, meek and lowly among the Pharisees and chief priests. Wherefore I ask you, my son, for love of him, to take pity with me on this little sheep, and let us pay the price and get her out from among these goats."

And brother Paul, wondering at his grief, began to grieve with him. But they had nothing but the poor tunics they wore, and as they were anxiously considering how the price might be paid, a merchant who was on a journey came up, and offered the price they desired. They took the sheep, giving thanks to God and came to Osimo, and went in to the bishop of that city, who received them with great reverence.

First Life of St Francis, 77, 78, 1228, Thomas of Celano

DIY recycling activity
a bee and butterfly garden

- You don't need a garden for this, but if you have, then dream big!

- Fill a large washing up bowl or equivalent with soil. Scatter and cover marigold, daisy, cornflower and poppy seeds. Keep them watered and watch them grow. These flowers are all self-seeding, so each year, they will look more beautiful.

- Plant lavender, if you have space.

See, judge and act

More than sixty per cent of all the plastic we use goes to landfill, is incinerated – ends up damaging our environment, oceans and marine life. Over one million marine animals (including mammals, fish, sharks, turtles and birds) are killed each year due to plastic debris in the ocean.

Instead of buying many small bottles of shampoo, shower gel, washing up liquid, kitchen cleaners, etc. buy a large container and refill your bottles. You'll save money and use less plastic.

DAY TWENTY-FOUR

RECOVER BEAUTY

Pope Francis

One of the Family, 1880, George Cotman

We have the freedom needed to limit and direct technology; we can put it at the service of another type of progress, one which is healthier, more human, more social, more integral. Liberation from the dominant technocratic paradigm does in fact happen sometimes, for example, when cooperatives of small producers adopt less polluting means of production, and opt for a non-consumerist model of life, recreation and community. Or when technology is directed primarily to resolving people's concrete problems, truly helping them live with more dignity and less suffering. Or indeed when the desire to create and contemplate beauty manages to overcome reductionism through a kind of salvation which occurs in beauty and in those who behold it. An authentic humanity, calling for a new synthesis, seems to dwell in the midst of our technological culture, almost unnoticed, like a mist seeping gently beneath a closed door. Will the promise last, in spite of everything, with all that is authentic rising up in stubborn resistance?

There is also the fact that people no longer seem to believe in a happy future; they no longer have blind trust in a better tomorrow based on the present state of the world and our technical abilities. There is a growing awareness that scientific and technological progress cannot be equated with the progress of humanity and history, a growing sense that the way to a better future lies elsewhere. This is not to reject the possibilities which technology continues to offer us. But humanity has changed profoundly, and the accumulation of constant novelties exalts a superficiality which pulls us in one direction. It becomes difficult to pause and recover depth in life. If architecture reflects the spirit of an age, our megastructures and drab apartment blocks express the spirit of globalized technology, where a constant flood of new products coexists with a tedious monotony. Let us refuse to resign ourselves to this and continue to wonder about the purpose and meaning of everything.

Laudato Si': on care for our common home:112-113, 2015, Pope Francis

REFLECTION

The Covid-19 pandemic showed us the advantages and disadvantages of technology. On the one hand, vaccines were created and distributed in record time. On the other, families appealed for help with home schooling, often online and inaccessible to households with no computer or internet access and insufficient money to access the technology which higher income families took for granted. Yet, many discovered freedom in disconnecting from computers and reconnecting with the natural world.

The Way Through the Woods

They shut the road through the woods
Seventy years ago.
Weather and rain have undone it again,
And now you would never know
There was once a path through the woods
Before they planted the trees:
It is underneath the coppice and heath,
And the thin anemones.
Only the keeper sees
That, where the ring-dove broods
And the badgers roll at ease,
There was once a road through the woods.

Yet, if you enter the woods
Of a summer evening late,
When the night-air cools on the trout-ring'd pools
Where the otter whistles his mate
(They fear not men in the woods
Because they see so few),
You will hear the beat of a horse's feet
And the swish of a skirt in the dew,
Steadily cantering through
The misty solitudes,

As though they perfectly knew
The old lost road through the woods ...
But there is no road through the woods.

Rudyard Kipling (1865-1936)

St Francis

Who could ever express the height of the affection by which [St Francis] was carried away as concerning all the things that are God's? Who could tell the sweetness which he enjoyed in contemplating in his creatures the wisdom, power and goodness of the Creator? Truly such thoughts often filled him with wondrous and unspeakable joy as he beheld the sun, or raised his eyes to the moon, or gazed on the stars, and the firmament. O simple piety! O pious simplicity! Even towards little worms he glowed with exceeding love, because he had read that word concerning the Saviour, "I am a worm, and no man." Wherefore he used to pick them up in the way and put them in a safe place, that they might not be crushed by the feet of passers-by. What shall I say of other lower creatures, when in winter he would cause honey or the best wine to be provided for bees, that they might not perish from cold? And he used to extol, to the glory of the Lord, the efficacy of their works and the excellence of their skill with such abundant utterance that many times he would pass a day in praise of them and of the other creatures.

First Life of St Francis, 80,1228, Thomas of Celano

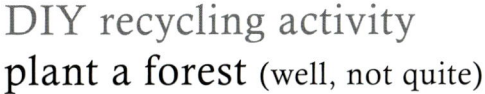

DIY recycling activity
plant a forest (well, not quite)

- When they are available, collect conkers, sycamore wings, hazelnuts, beechnuts, etc. In the spring, plant them in a pot or larger planter and keep them watered.
- Enjoy the seedlings, even on the kitchen windowsill.
- When the seedlings are too big for convenience, plant them outdoors, perhaps in a wooded area or in your garden, where they can grow big and beautiful.

See, judge and act

Batteries carry a risk of giving off toxic gases if damaged, but core ingredients such as lithium and cobalt are finite resources. Extraction of the metals uses water supplies and can also cause water pollution. Dumping of batteries in non-recyclable rubbish means that they go to landfill, gradually break down and eventually pollute the environment.

Recycle your old batteries. Many supermarkets, public libraries and other places act as collection points.

Consider buying rechargeable AA and AAA batteries. Sometimes the rechargeable batteries supply power for longer than the non-rechargeable ones.

DAY TWENTY-FIVE

RESTORE THE NATURAL WORLD *AND* HUMANITY

Pope Francis

Ethiopia: serving Somali refugees, © Jesuit Refugee Service

The time has come to pay renewed attention to reality and the limits it imposes; this in turn is the condition for a more sound and fruitful development of individuals and society…

Neglecting to monitor the harm done to nature and the environmental impact of our decisions is only the most striking sign of a disregard for the message contained in the structures of nature itself. When we fail to acknowledge as part of reality the worth of a poor person, a human embryo, a person with disabilities – to offer just a few examples – it becomes difficult to hear the cry of nature itself; everything is connected. Once the human being declares independence from reality and behaves with absolute dominion, the very foundations of our life begin to crumble, for "instead of carrying out his role as a co-operator with God in the work of creation, man sets himself up in place of God and thus ends up provoking a rebellion on the part of nature".

This situation has led to a constant schizophrenia, wherein a technocracy which sees no intrinsic value in lesser beings coexists with the other extreme, which sees no special value in human beings… There can be no renewal of our relationship with nature without a renewal of humanity itself. There can be no ecology without an adequate anthropology. When the human person is considered as simply one being among others, the product of chance or physical determinism, then "our overall sense of responsibility wanes…" Human beings cannot be expected to feel responsibility for the world unless, at the same time, their unique capacities of knowledge, will, freedom and responsibility are recognised and valued.

Laudato Si': on care for our common home:116-118, 2015, Pope Francis

REFLECTION

When a simple treadle sewing machine can transform the lives of everybody in the village, why would someone want a sports car which gets stuck at the traffic lights?

A Minor Bird

I have wished a bird would fly away,
And not sing by my house all day;

Have clapped my hands at him from the door
When it seemed as if I could bear no more.

The fault must partly have been in me.
The bird was not to blame for his key.

And of course there must be something wrong
In wanting to silence any song.

Robert Frost (1874-1963)

St Francis

What gladness do you think the beauty of flowers afforded to his mind as he observed the grace of their form and perceived the sweetness of their perfume? For he turned forthwith the eye of consideration to the beauty of that Flower which, brightly coming forth in springtime from the root of Jesse, has by its perfume raised up countless thousands of the dead. And when he came upon a quantity of flowers, he would preach to them and invite them to praise the Lord, just as if they had been gifted with reason. So also, cornfields, and vineyards, stones, woods, and all the beauties of the field, fountains of waters, all the verdure of gardens, earth, and fire, air and wind would he with sincerest purity exhort to the love and willing service of God. In short he called all creatures by the name of brother, and in a surpassing manner, of which other men had no experience, he discerned the hidden things of creation with the eye of the heart, as one who had already escaped into the glorious liberty of the children of God.

First Life of St Francis, 81, 82,1228, Thomas of Celano

DIY recycling activity
a sweetcorn crop

- Take a fresh corncob and place in a bowl of water until, after a few days, the individual grains start to send out shoots. Empty out the water and fill the bowl with soil, covering the new shoots. Keep the soil moist.

- When the shoots are big enough, separate them out and plant outdoors, perhaps in your garden as maize plants are tall.

See, judge and act

Grow geraniums – indoors and/or outdoors. They like poor soil, take little water, grow easily, naturally repel mosquitos, are often scented, and are bright and colourful. Cuttings also grow easily. There are hundreds of different varieties, so take your pick!

DAY TWENTY-SIX

ATTITUDES TO WORK AFFECT THE ENVIRONMENT

Pope Francis

If we reflect on the proper relationship between human beings and the world around us, we see the need for a correct understanding of work; if we talk about the relationship between human beings and things, the question arises as to the meaning and purpose of all human activity. This has to do not only with manual or agricultural labour but with any activity involving a modification of existing reality, from producing a social report to the design of a technological development. Underlying every form of work is a concept of the relationship which we can and must have with what is other than ourselves. Together with the awe-filled contemplation of creation which we find in St Francis of Assisi, the Christian spiritual tradition has also developed a rich and balanced understanding of the meaning of work, as, for example, in the life of Blessed Charles de Foucauld and his followers.

We can also look to the great tradition of monasticism. Originally, it was a kind of flight from the world, an escape from the decadence of the cities. The monks sought the desert, convinced that it was the best place for encountering the presence of God. Later, St Benedict of Norcia proposed that his monks live in community, combining prayer and spiritual reading with manual labour (*ora et labora*). Seeing manual labour as spiritually meaningful proved revolutionary. Personal

The Angelus, 1857-59, Jean-Francois Millet

growth and sanctification came to be sought in the interplay of recollection and work. This way of experiencing work makes us more protective and respectful of the environment; it imbues our relationship to the world with a healthy sobriety.

We are convinced that "man is the source, the focus and the aim of all economic and social life". Nonetheless, once our human capacity for contemplation and reverence is impaired, it becomes easy for the meaning of work to be misunderstood. We need to remember that men and women have "the capacity to improve their lot, to further their moral growth and to develop their spiritual endowments". Work should be the setting for this rich personal growth, where many aspects of life enter into play: creativity, planning for the future, developing our talents, living out our values, relating to others, giving glory to God. It follows that, in the reality of today's global society, it is essential that "we continue to prioritize the goal of access to steady employment for everyone", no matter the limited interests of business and dubious economic reasoning.

Laudato Si': on care for our common home:125-127, 2015, Pope Francis

REFLECTION

Then a ploughman said, Speak to us of Work.

And he answered, saying: You work that you may keep pace with the earth and the soul of the earth.

For to be idle is to become a stranger unto the seasons, and to step out of life's procession, that marches in majesty and proud submission towards the infinite.

When you work you are a flute through whose heart the whispering of the hours turns to music.

Which of you would be a reed, dumb and silent, when all else sings together in unison?

Always you have been told that work is a curse and labour a misfortune.

But I say to you that when you work you fulfil a part of earth's furthest dream, assigned to you when the dream was born,

And in keeping yourself with labour you are in truth loving life,

And to love life through labour is to be intimate with life's inmost secret.

Kahlil Gibran (1883-1931)

Leisure

What is this life if, full of care,
We have no time to stand and stare

No time to stand beneath the boughs,
And stare as long as sheep and cows

No time to see, when woods we pass,
Where squirrels hide their nuts in grass

No time to see, in broad daylight,
Streams full of stars, like skies at night

No time to turn at Beauty's glance,
And watch her feet, how they can dance
No time to wait till her mouth can
Enrich that smile her eyes began

A poor life this if, full of care,
We have no time to stand and stare.

W. H. Davies (1871-1940)

St Francis

When he was walking with a certain Brother through the Venetian marshes, he chanced on a great host of birds that were sitting and singing among the bushes. Seeing them, he said unto his companion: "Our sisters the birds are praising their Creator, let us too go among them and sing unto the Lord praises and the canonical Hours." When they had gone into their midst, the birds stirred not from the spot, and when, by reason of their twittering, they could not hear each the other in reciting the Hours, the holy man turned unto the birds, saying: "My sisters the birds, cease from singing, while that we render our due praises unto the Lord." Then the birds forthwith held their peace, and remained silent until, having said his Hours at leisure and rendered his praises, the holy man of God again gave them leave to sing. And, as the man of God gave them leave, they at once took up their song again after their wonted fashion.

The Life of St Francis of Assisi, 9, 1263, St Bonaventure

DIY recycling activity
water relay race

- Each team is given an identical container filled to the brim with the same amount of water.
- Set a clear start and finishing point.
- Children take it in turns to run to the finishing point, go back to the team, hand over the container of water to the next person.
- The winning team is the one which has the most water in their container.

See, judge and act

Leaving electrical equipment on standby wastes electricity as they still use power, albeit at a lower rate. Have you noticed that plugs are often still warm even when the appliance is only on standby?

Before you go to bed, remember to switch off electrical equipment and close down your computer. You probably don't need them all on standby while you are sleeping.

DAY TWENTY-SEVEN

WORK IS A VOCATION
Pope Francis

Shipbuilders, dockside frieze, Liverpool,
© Sr Janet Fearns

We were created with a vocation to work. The goal should not be that technological progress increasingly replace human work, for this would be detrimental to humanity. Work is a necessity, part of the meaning of life on this earth, a path to growth, human development and personal fulfilment. Helping the poor financially must always be a provisional solution in the face of pressing needs. The broader objective should always be to allow them a dignified life through work. Yet the orientation of the economy has favoured a kind of technological progress in which the costs of production are reduced by laying off workers and replacing them with machines. This is yet another way in which we can end up working against ourselves. The loss of jobs also has a negative impact on the economy "through the progressive erosion of social capital: the network of relationships of trust, dependability, and respect for rules, all of which are indispensable for any form of civil coexistence". In other words, "human costs always include economic costs, and economic dysfunctions always involve human costs". To stop investing in people, in order to gain greater short-term financial gain, is bad business for society.

In order to continue providing employment, it is imperative to promote an economy which favours productive diversity and business creativity. For example, there is a great variety of small-scale food production systems which feed the greater part of the world's peoples, using a modest amount of land and producing less waste, be it in small agricultural parcels, in orchards and gardens, hunting and wild harvesting or local fishing.

Economies of scale, especially in the agricultural sector, end up forcing smallholders to sell their land or to abandon their traditional crops. Their attempts to move to other, more diversified, means of production prove fruitless because of the difficulty of linkage with regional and global markets, or because the infrastructure for sales and transport is geared to larger businesses. Civil authorities have the right and duty to adopt clear and firm measures in support of small producers and differentiated production. To ensure economic freedom from which all can effectively benefit, restraints occasionally have to be imposed on those possessing greater resources and financial power. To claim economic freedom while real conditions bar many people from actual access to it, and while possibilities for employment continue to shrink, is to practise a doublespeak which brings politics into disrepute. Business is a noble vocation, directed to producing wealth and improving our world. It can be a fruitful source of prosperity for the areas in which it operates, especially if it sees the creation of jobs as an essential part of its service to the common good.

Laudato Si': on care for our common home:128-129, 2015, Pope Francis

REFLECTION

And all work is empty save when there is love;

And when you work with love you bind yourself to yourself, and to one another, and to God.

And what is it to work with love?

It is to weave the cloth with threads drawn from your heart, even as if your beloved were to wear that cloth.

It is to build a house with affection, even as if your beloved were to dwell in that house.

It is to sow seeds with tenderness and reap the harvest with joy, even as if your beloved were to eat the fruit.

It is to charge all things you fashion with a breath of your own spirit.

And to know that all the blessed dead are standing about you and watching.

Often have I heard you say, as if speaking in sleep, "He who works in marble, and finds the shape of his own soul in the stone, is nobler than he who ploughs the soil.

And he who seizes the rainbow to lay it on a cloth in the likeness of man, is more than he who makes the sandals for our feet."

But I say, not in sleep but in the overwakefulness of noontide, that the wind speaks not more sweetly to the giant oaks than to the least of all the blades of grass;

And he alone is great who turns the voice of the wind into a song made sweeter by his own loving.

Work is love made visible.

And if you cannot work with love but only with distaste, it is better that you should leave your work and sit at the gate of the temple and take alms of those who work with joy.

For if you bake bread with indifference, you bake a bitter bread that feeds but half man's hunger.

And if you grudge the crushing of the grapes, your grudge distils a poison in the wine.

And if you sing though as angels, and love not the singing, you muffle man's ears to the voices of the day and the voices of the night.

Kahlil Gibran (1883-1931)

My Wage

I bargained with Life for a penny,
And Life would pay no more,
However, I begged at evening
When I counted my scanty store;

For Life is a just employer,
He gives you what you ask,
But once you have set the wages,
Why, you must bear the task.

I worked for a menial's hire,
Only to learn, dismayed,
That any wage I had asked of Life,
Life would have paid.

Jessie B. Rittenhouse (1869-1948)

St Francis

And then the holy lover of all humility betook him to the lepers, and was with them, serving them all most zealously for God's sake, washing all foulness from them and even wiping away the matter from the ulcers; even as he says himself in his Testament, "For when I was in sin it seemed to me exceeding bitter to look on lepers, but the Lord brought me among them, and I showed mercy unto them." For indeed at one time the sight of lepers was (as he used to say) so bitter to him that when in the days of his vanity he looked at their houses about two miles off, he stopped his nostrils with his hands. But when now by the grace and power of the Highest he was beginning to think of holy and profitable things, one day, while still in the habit of the world, he met a leper, and, having become stronger than himself, went near and kissed him.

First Life of St Francis, 17,1228, Thomas of Celano

DIY recycling activity
DIY jigsaw puzzle

- Make jigsaw pieces by cutting up the side of a cereal box. Jumble up the pieces and reassemble them.

- When the game is over, recycle the cardboard.

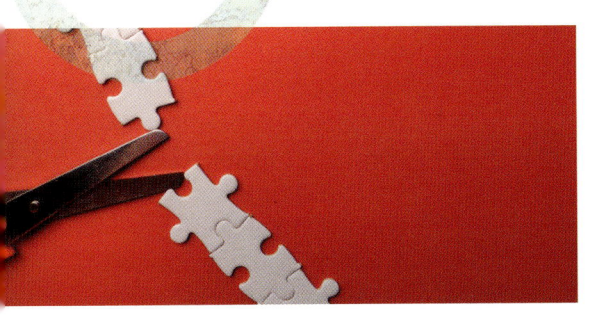

See, judge and act

Seasonal fruit and vegetables are often locally grown and travel shorter distances before they reach us. Meat production releases more greenhouse gases such as methane, CO_2, and nitrous oxide.

Where it is feasible, healthy and practical, try to eat a meat-free meal each day.

DAY TWENTY-EIGHT

EVERYTHING IS INTERCONNECTED
Pope Francis

Ecology studies the relationship between living organisms and the environment in which they develop. This necessarily entails reflection and debate about the conditions required for the life and survival of society, and the honesty needed to question certain models of development, production and consumption. It cannot be emphasized enough how everything is interconnected. Time and space are not independent of one another, and not even atoms or subatomic particles can be considered in isolation. Just as the different aspects of the planet – physical, chemical and biological – are interrelated, so too living species are part of a network which we will never fully explore and understand. A good part of our genetic code is shared by many living beings. It follows that the fragmentation of knowledge and the isolation of bits of information can actually become a form of ignorance, unless they are integrated into a broader vision of reality.

St Francis, children and doves, Rivo Torto, Assisi, © Sr Janet Fearns

When we speak of the "environment", what we really mean is a relationship existing between nature and the society which lives in it. Nature cannot be regarded as something separate from ourselves or as a mere setting in which we live. We are part of nature, included in it and thus in constant interaction with it. Recognising the reasons why a given area is polluted requires a study of the workings of society, its economy, its behaviour patterns, and the ways it grasps reality. Given the scale of change, it is no longer possible to find a specific, discrete answer for each part of the problem. It is essential to seek comprehensive solutions which consider the interactions within natural systems themselves and with social systems. We are faced not with two separate crises, one environmental and the other social, but rather with one complex crisis which is both social and environmental. Strategies for a solution demand an integrated approach to combating poverty, restoring dignity to the excluded, and at the same time protecting nature.

Laudato Si': on care for our common home:138,139, 2015, Pope Francis

REFLECTION

When we look at the world around us, do we see it with the eyes of a child: full of wonder, beauty and adventure, or with the tired eyes of a stressed adult, seeing the loveliness but also the broken fences, leaking taps and potholes?

On a Lane in Spring

A little lane – the brook runs close beside,
And spangles in the sunshine, while the fish glide swiftly by;
And hedges leafing with the green springtide;
From out their greenery the old birds fly,
And chirp and whistle in the morning sun;
The pilewort glitters 'neath the pale blue sky,
The little robin has its nest begun
The grass-green linnets round the bushes fly.
How mild the spring comes in! the daisy buds
Lift up their golden blossoms to the sky.
How lovely are the pingles* and the woods!
Here a beetle runs – and there a fly
Rests on the arum leaf in bottle-green,
And all the spring in this sweet lane is seen.

John Clare (1793-1864)

* Pingle: *A small enclosed piece of land; a paddock.*

St Francis

Surely at that time St Francis and his brethren did singularly exult and exceedingly rejoice when any faithful man among the Christian people, whosoever or of what quality so ever he might be, rich, poor, noble, low-born, despised, valued, wise, simple, clerk, unlettered, or layman came, led by the Spirit of God, to receive the habit of holy Religion. Men of the world also wondered greatly at all these things, and the example of humility provoked them to amend their way of life and repent of their sins. Neither low birth nor the drawback of poverty was any obstacle to his building up in the work of God those that it was the will of God to build up, who delights to be with the simple, and the outcasts of the world.

First Life of St Francis, 31,1228, Thomas of Celano

DIY recycling activity
grow a banana

- Slice a banana in half and, with a teaspoon, scrape off the seeds. Plant them in soil – perhaps on a windowsill – and watch your banana plants grow. They will eventually grow too big for a windowsill and will need to be transplanted where they are unlikely to experience frostbite.

See, judge and act

Heating makes up forty per cent of the UK's energy consumption.

Where it is feasible, healthy and practical, try to run your central heating 1°C cooler than usual. You probably won't notice the drop in temperature, but your fuel bill – and the planet – will see the difference.

DAY TWENTY-NINE

SAFEGUARD CULTURE
Pope Francis

Building a thatched roof, South Sudan, © Jesuit Refugee Service

Together with the patrimony of nature, there is also an historic, artistic and cultural patrimony which is likewise under threat… there is a need to incorporate the history, culture and architecture of each place, thus preserving its original identity. Ecology, then, also involves protecting the cultural treasures of humanity in the broadest sense… Culture is more than what we have inherited from the past; it is also, and above all, a living, dynamic and participatory present reality, which cannot be excluded as we rethink the relationship between human beings and the environment…

New processes taking shape cannot always fit into frameworks imported from outside; they need to be based in the local culture itself… Nor can the notion of the quality of life be imposed from without, for quality of life must be understood within the world of symbols and customs proper to each human group…

The disappearance of a culture can be just as serious, or even more serious, than the disappearance of a species of plant or animal.

In this sense, it is essential to show special care for indigenous communities and their cultural traditions. They are not merely one minority among others, but should be the principal dialogue partners, especially when large projects affecting their land are proposed. For them, land is not a commodity but rather a gift from God and from their ancestors who rest there, a sacred space with which they need to interact if they are to maintain their identity and values. When they remain on their land, they themselves care for it best. Nevertheless, in various parts of the world, pressure is being put on them to abandon their homelands to make room for agricultural or mining projects which are undertaken without regard for the degradation of nature and culture.

Laudato Si': on care for our common home:143-146, 2015, Pope Francis

REFLECTION

Most of us don't recognise the huge richness of our cultural heritage until we find ourselves within a different cultural setting, perhaps in another country or language area. Even within our own country, local expressions which are easily understood often make little or no sense elsewhere – so imagine what it is like for refugees and "displaced persons" who find themselves in a foreign land with little or no shared history. Suddenly, they must forge a new present and a new future together but, initially on split levels. There's a big difference between the host and the recipient of charity. It's tough when circumstances, accidentally or deliberately, enforce new ways of thinking and speaking.

Poverty

I hate this grinding poverty –
To toil, and pinch, and borrow,
And be for ever haunted by
The spectre of to-morrow.
It breaks the strong heart of a man,
It crushes out his spirit –
Do what he will, do what he can,
However high his merit!

I hate the praise that Want has got
From preacher and from poet,
The cant of those who know it not
To blind the men who know it.
The greatest curse since man had birth,
An everlasting terror:
The cause of half the crime on earth,
The cause of half the error.

Henry Lawson (1867-1922)

St Francis

Francis, the poor man, the father of the poor, making himself like unto the poor in all things, used to be distressed to see any one poorer than himself, not because he coveted vain renown, but only from a feeling of sympathy; and though he was content with a very common and rough tunic, he often longed to share it with some poor man. But in order that this richest of poor men, led by his great feeling of tenderness, might (in whatsoever way) help the poor, he would in very cold weather ask the rich of this world to lend him a mantle of furs. When in their devotion they complied with his request even more readily than he had made it, he would say to them, "I will take this from you on the understanding that you do not expect to have it back any more," and then with joy and exultation he would clothe the first poor man he met with whatever had been given him. He was very much distressed if he saw any poor man harshly spoken to, or if he heard anyone utter a curse against any creature.

For instance, it happened that a brother had given a sharp answer to a poor man who had asked alms, saying, "See to it, for perhaps you are a rich man feigning poverty". When St Francis, the father of the poor, heard of it he was deeply grieved, and sharply rebuked the brother who had spoken thus, and bade him strip himself before the poor man, kiss his feet and beg his pardon. For he used to say, "He who reviles a poor man does a wrong to Christ, for the poor man bears the noble ensign of Christ who made himself poor in this world for us". Often therefore when he found poor people laden with wood or other burdens, he would help them by giving the support of his own shoulders, even though very weak.

First Life of St Francis, 76,1228, Thomas of Celano

DIY recycling activity
pack a pallet

Half-bury a wooden pallet in soil. Get the children to find and plant different seeds in each section. This tests their ingenuity and can also have spectacularly colourful results. The slats clearly mark each section so that this activity can also be a competition involving several children.

See, judge and act

Tea farmers and workers struggle to get a fair deal. They and their children are often malnourished, illiterate and survive on less than $2 per day.

Buy from producers whom you know strive to act justly towards their employees and pay a living wage.

DAY THIRTY

RESPECT QUALITY OF LIFE
Pope Francis

There is also a need to protect those common areas, visual landmarks and urban landscapes which increase our sense of belonging, of rootedness, of "feeling at home" within a city which includes us and brings us together. It is important that the different parts of a city be well integrated and that those who live there have a sense of the whole, rather than being confined to one neighbourhood and failing to see the larger city as space which they share with others…

Lack of housing is a grave problem in many parts of the world, both in rural areas and in large cities, since state budgets usually cover only a small portion of the demand. Not only the poor, but many other members of society as well, find it difficult to own a home. Having a home has much to do with a sense of personal dignity and the growth of families. This is a major issue for human ecology. In some places, where makeshift shanty towns have sprung up, this will mean developing those neighbourhoods rather than razing or displacing them…

The quality of life in cities has much to do with systems of transport, which are often a source of much suffering for those who

Eastern Aleppo,
© Jesuit Refugee Service

use them. Many cars, used by one or more people, circulate in cities, causing traffic congestion, raising the level of pollution, and consuming enormous quantities of non-renewable energy. This makes it necessary to build more roads and parking areas which spoil the urban landscape. Many specialists agree on the need to give priority to public transportation. Yet some measures needed will not prove easily acceptable to society unless substantial improvements are made in the systems themselves, which in many cities force people to put up with undignified conditions due to crowding, inconvenience, infrequent service and lack of safety.

Respect for our dignity as human beings often jars with the chaotic realities that people have to endure in city life. Yet this should not make us overlook the abandonment and neglect also experienced by some rural populations which lack access to essential services and where some workers are reduced to conditions of servitude, without rights or even the hope of a more dignified life.

Laudato Si': on care for our common home:151-154, 2015, Pope Francis

REFLECTION

The streets of a city are not paved with gold. Far from it! In many shanty towns, people live in appalling conditions and yet survive with amazing dignity and self-respect. A family's entire wardrobe might be contained in a few plastic carrier bags hung on nails hammered into the wall of one room, and yet on Sunday, when they go to church, even the poorest clothing is freshly-washed, ironed, sparkling and worn as if it were the latest creation of a top fashion designer.

Many shanty compound dwellers save up to buy a single bar of soap. Yet, if a neighbour is too sick to leave their bed, in an act of incredible generosity, they will often use that precious bar of soap to wash the soiled bedding.

Such people show that, with support, even the most apparently hopeless situations can be hope-filled.

The Poor

I walk the streets and though not meanly drest,
Yet none so poor as can with me compare;
For none though weary call me into rest,
And though I hunger, none their substance share;
I ask not for my stay the broken reed,
That fails when most I want a friendly arm;
I cannot on the loaves and fishes feed
That want the blessing that they may not harm;
I only ask the living word to hear
From tongues that now but speak to utter death;
I thirst for one cool cup of water clear
But drink the riled stream of lying breath;
And wander on though in my Fatherland,
Yet hear no welcome voice and see no beckoning hand.

Jones Very (1813-80)

St Francis

There should not be any brother in the world who has sinned, however much he may have possibly sinned, who, after he has looked into your eyes, would go away without having received your mercy, if he is looking for mercy. And if he were not to seek mercy, you should ask him if he wants mercy. And if he should sin thereafter a thousand times before your very eyes, love him more than me so that you may draw him back to the Lord. Always be merciful to brothers such as these.

Letter to a Minister, 1221-23, St Francis

DIY recycling activity
create your own Easter garden

- Place a plant pot on its side on a tray or large flat dish. Cover half of the tray and plant pot with soil or moss, making a hill and a tomb. Scatter gravel in front of the tomb. If the soil is deep enough, you might like to plant primroses or other small flowers.

- A flat stone inside the plant pot will help to keep it stable and will also act as the slab on which the body of Jesus was laid.

- Using twigs or string, make three crosses and place them in the soil.

- Fold two small pieces of white cloth and place them on the stone inside the plant pot. These represent the cloths which were used to wrap the body of Jesus.

- Close the entrance to the tomb with a large flat stone which you can move to the side on Easter Sunday to show that Jesus has risen.

See, judge and act

Much of our food is carried from its place of origin to our shops, often travelling between countries. Growing your own means that the distance travelled by your food can be as short as from the windowsill to the kitchen worktop. It's a wonderful way of feeding yourself and eliminating the greenhouse gases produced by commercial transport.

Buy a gro-bag and grow your own tomatoes.

ADDED EXTRA

A Prayer for our Earth

All-powerful God, you are present in the whole universe
and in the smallest of your creatures.
You embrace with your tenderness all that exists.
Pour out upon us the power of your love,
that we may protect life and beauty.
Fill us with peace, that we may live
as brothers and sisters, harming no one.
O God of the poor,
help us to rescue the abandoned and forgotten of this earth,
so precious in your eyes.
Bring healing to our lives,
that we may protect the world and not prey on it,
that we may sow beauty, not pollution and destruction.
Touch the hearts
of those who look only for gain
at the expense of the poor and the earth.
Teach us to discover the worth of each thing,
to be filled with awe and contemplation,
to recognize that we are profoundly united
with every creature
as we journey towards your infinite light.
We thank you for being with us each day.
Encourage us, we pray, in our struggle
for justice, love and peace.

Laudato Si': on care for our common home: 246, 2015, Pope Francis

Prayers from the Garden

Lord, let us see ourselves as
  others see us
So we might know our faults.
Let us see ourselves in others
So we may know what pleases.
Let us look on others as
  brothers and sisters
That we may know truth.
Let us stand before you as
  honest children
That we may be open
  at all times.
Let us greet all with openness

That we might know friendship.
Let us be centred
  on a love for you
That we will not know division.
Let us realise that you
  hold all of us dear
That we can do the same.
Lord, stand next to us
That we may know you
  in all we meet.
Give us grace to share your
  presence
In our every meeting.
Amen.

Let me trust in thee
That I may safely see
All thou hast prepared
In this life for me.

Grant me grace to know
The debt to thee I owe
Has been fully paid
By One who loves me so.

Take my love on trust
Giving it as I must
Your love its own reward:
The diamond in the dust.

Let me trust to time
As all I am is thine
That I may be refined.
In thee my life does shine.

May the sun be in our day
To light all that glorifies God.
May the wind make flowers sway
To move to the rhythms of God.
May rain fall early and late
To slake our daily thirst.
May hands open the gate
The same, last or first.
May eyes see God in all
To wonder at his garden fair.
May hearts responding call
To praise that love we share.
Amen.

Heavenly Father, help us to use the past to shape the future.
Grant wisdom to recognise past mistakes and to learn from them.
Grant strength to use them to build a life anew in Your image.
Grant time to understand how to grow in faith.
Grant vision so that I can see the good
    that comes from reflection and redemption.
Grant the joy of being in Your presence while I contemplate my life.
Grant grace to understand how I might grow in Your company.
Amen.

When I see all those turns in the road
It's then that you make it straight;
When I see bends that never end
You won't let me falter or wait;
For it's you who can guide me through
All those miles when I am alone;
I know you are there by my side
For you would never leave me on my own;
When I see all those turns in the road
There is something that I have to pray;
Just as you led me through
Let me lead others along your Way.
Amen.

Help us not to
    labour in vain.
Help us through
    life's changes.
Help us when we
    have no other help.
Help us when our
    work seems hard.
Help us to labour
    in your name.
Help us to be
    grateful for
    your miracles.
Amen.

Lord, help me be the person you want me to be.
Help me recognise the gifts you have given me.
Help me to know how I may use them.
Help me to do this to your glory.
Help me to realise their effect on others.
Help me to know your message in all I do.
Help me to understand.
Help me to share what you freely give
    so your gifts may not be wasted nor withheld.
Help the person you want to be me to be me.
Amen.

© Clifford Birchall

MIGHTY OAKS

Elzéard Bouffier was a French shepherd and widower who lived in an Alpine valley which loggers had ruined and its original inhabitants had abandoned.

Bouffier decided to bring life back to his valley and home and so, every day, the lonely shepherd walked several miles to the nearest forest in order to collect fallen acorns from the forest floor. Every day, he returned to his cottage, dug holes in the ground and planted the acorns.

Replanting the forest took many years but, acorn by acorn, the barrenness gave way to green shoots, slender saplings and trees. Water once again flowed in the dried-up river bed. People returned and built new homes. The sounds of birdsong and children's laughter came back to fill the empty silence.

"Mighty oaks from little acorns grow." Sometimes we just need a little bit of hope and buckets of perseverance.

The tale of Elzéard Bouffier was told by Jean Giono in a short story, The Man who Planted Trees, which later became a film of the same title.

Previously published in Advent Extra 2020

REACH FOR A STAR

"That's Mummy's star. It's there so that every time you look at it you can say hello and you can say a prayer for her."

The death of a loved one is achingly lonely. It can be very hard for a small child – and incredibly painful for whoever is supporting them. It's almost impossible to be "brave" with a broken heart.

Try using an easily identifiable star as a point of contact. Whether it's a star or a planet doesn't matter: it becomes "Mummy's star" or whosoever it is whom you long to be near again. Seeing that friendly star, night after night, can help to fill the bottomless hole in your hearts.

Let the star's light comfort you and remind you of someone who helped to make life worth living. If you want, have a good cry. The star isn't the person you love so much, but it can be a valuable link. Use it to pray to and for someone who was uniquely precious. Remember the very special times you shared – re-live and treasure them.

REWILDING THE WORLD

Natural historian Mary Colwell witnessed the before and aftereffects of the pandemic on the natural world and rejoiced in the difference

In January I visited Venice. The beauty of the buildings, the rich cultural life, and the sense that God is honoured around every corner, was overwhelming. I visited the opera, galleries, restaurants and I spent two evenings rapt by sacred choral music performed in ornate chapels whose walls were priceless works of art. As an expression of ecclesiastical majesty and human genius, Venice is, beyond question, a wonder of the world.

Yet – I yearned for a green space. I searched for quiet groves where I could gather my thoughts, where the sweet music of birds could enhance my contemplation on the mysteries made manifest in sculpture, paintings and music. I could not find any. I also crouched on the steps that led into the water of the canals to try to spot fish.

Their gentle movements in a medium I cannot inhabit always brings a different perspective to human environments. I love to watch fish, they are a connection to deep time, to the eons before mammals walked on dry land and when water held all of the life on earth. They have played a central role in human history, and today they provide nearly one-fifth of the protein we eat. I like to think of them as silent witnesses to when, "The earth was without form and void, and darkness was over the face of the deep. And the Spirit of God was hovering over the face of the waters." But I couldn't see them in Venice's famed canals. The water was too murky with silt, churned up by the motorboats that constantly cruise the narrow channels. If they were there, they were hidden in darkness.

Deer in London by Xinhua/shutterstock_editorial_10607437g

Taking a trip to the islands in the lagoon, I noticed how badly eroded their coastlines have become as precious sediment is swept away by the waves caused by the water taxis and cruisers. The soft, shifting boundaries between land and water are badly damaged and degraded. The vegetation, so vital as nurseries for small fish and other sea life, is threadbare and barely holding fast.

Reflecting on my time in *La Serenissima*, I concluded that the connection between God and humanity is gloriously celebrated in art and architecture, but recognition of that vital relationship between the creator and the natural world was nowhere to be seen.

Just weeks later, everything changed. Venice, like most of world, was gripped by the chaos of the pandemic. The busy streets became quiet and the boats moored. At last the waters were stilled. It was then that the fish appeared in the canals. They swam in glittering light and glided in an out of the seaweed that waved above a now visible sandy base. Jelly fish pulsated and glimmered, like glass ornaments come alive. The blue sky and white clouds were reflected in crystalline waters. Cormorants appeared to feed on fish they could now see. Dolphins were regularly spotted in the lagoon. After just a few weeks, nature returned to Venice.

The floating city was not alone. Soon, a litany of creaturely antics was recorded in newspapers and online. An otter family were photographed trotting past a hospital in Singapore, coyotes appeared in car parks in San Francisco, penguins waddled down streets in South Africa, kangaroos hopped across the roads in Adelaide, herds of deer rested on green verges in London, wild boar wandered over a zebra crossing in Israel and in Wales goats browsed in the centre of Llandudno.

The sudden appearance of wildlife was made possible by what has been coined the "circuit breaker effect," a disruption to normality that allows life to take advantage of our disappearance. Confined to our houses, we could only watch as the living planet frolicked and played outside. It was a glimpse of what life could be like if nature is given a breathing space.

The circuit breaker worked on many of us too. A common refrain during the lockdown was how much more people appreciated the nature that lived alongside them. Although it was always there, it had gone unnoticed in the busyness of life. In the weeks at home, for those with gardens, or who lived in rural places, the natural world seemed so much more vital. Birdsong entered our lives, cheering us through difficult days. Spring flowers bloomed brightly. Outside my house, with no council workers armed with pesticides, "weeds" grew up between the pavements creating an eclectic jumble of wild plants that attracted bees and butterflies. Wildlife took on an extra dimension, one of companion and fellow traveller. It provided a joy that required no subscription to enjoy, it was a gift freely given. Birds and butterflies, flowers and trees also gave us an anchor point in a world that was suddenly dangerous and challenging.

An American scientist friend wrote to me about her time in isolation. She would normally have been out in the wilds studying endangered birds and helping to protect them. It was frustrating for her as she has so much important work to do. Confined to walks around her town, however, she found unexpected peace. "For me, it has made me more aware and, ironically enough – though socially distanced – I feel more connected in many ways, especially this morning. It is in these gentle moments that I feel the closest to nature and I can truly breathe. I just now feel like I am breathing much deeper."

Gentle moments – a good phrase to describe a glimpse of grace. The reappearance of nature has given many of us grace-filled connections which I hope will continue as the world slowly returns to whatever the new normal will be. We may, of course, slide back into the rule of money. Or might we take a more natural path and learn from what we have been taught about our relationship with nature? I am moved to note the wisdom of the composer, Debussy. "Listen to no one's advice except that of the wind in the trees. That can recount the whole history of mankind…"

And we celebrate the Word who created that history and entered our world's beautiful, fragile loveliness…

Mary Colwell is an award-winning wildlife broadcaster, writer and environmental campaigner

Previously published in Advent Extra 2020

I SEE

"T" looks out of his cell window and sees, not the metal bars and barbed wire, but the glory of Creation. He looks at his fellow inmates and sees brothers whom Jesus loves.

I don't look at the barbed wire and brick walls.

I see the trees in the distance, standing tall.

The leaves on display, calling out, the branches calling out to the animals, "Come to me. I'll give you rest, I'll give you shelter, rest in me, I am strong and able to bear you, rest in me, make your nest in me".

The trees swaying so gently in the breeze,

One is still bare, still waiting to bloom.

It will come, it will come: all things have their season.

The nest at the top, the very top

Even on something so bare, life is still there.

Eggs waiting to hatch, or maybe they have already. Maybe they're just waiting to spread their wings to start their adventure that is life.

I don't look at the concrete and the metal railings.

I see patches of grass poking out from where it can, squeezing its way through, bursting through like a nature warrior.

I see the dandelions popping up, yes they have made it. That bright yellow in the corner,
so small yet undeniable…
nature prevails.

I don't look at the tin roof, the corrugated steel.

I see a place of worship, where souls are saved and hearts are uplifted, where men gather together in unity and give God the praise, the oh so beautiful praise.

I see a home to smiles, to friendships and brotherhoods, love for God, love for each other.

I don't see a metal sculpture. I see a beacon of hope, a ray of light, a reason to go on.

The cross stands there for all to see, "Come to me all who are weary and burdened and I will give you rest." Life it gives.

Does the sacrifice not show? What Jesus did, this is love I know.

I was in a cloud of darkness but he took it from me there.

I don't look at the cage on my cell or the window frame welded in.

I see the blue sky, covering the whole above.

Nothing escapes it, it is vast.

The blue sky sits so effortlessly, it sits with blue beauty.

It spreads far as far as the eye can see.

It enraptures me, nothing else is like it, nothing else.

I choose to see these things,

I choose to see the good,

I choose to live in hope.

As everyone should.

Previously published in Lent Extra 2021

KEEPING ON TRACK

The passage from darkness to light has special significance when at sea. During his 37 years in the Royal Navy, Ian Crabtree gained considerable experience and understanding of the importance of the watchman's role.

"Sunset, Sir!" "Make it so!" The opening commands of a centuries-old ceremonial act that takes place every night in a Royal Navy establishment and ship alongside when the White Ensign is lowered. At sea, sunset marks the time when the ship's navigation lights are switched on and the upper deck made secure. On a clear day with a good horizon, it is also the time when the Officer of the Watch on the Bridge checks the accuracy of the gyro by take a bearing of the lower limb of the sun when it is a semi-diameter above the horizon. As dusk descends, the Navigator will appear with his sextant ready to take star sights which he will use to fix the geographical position of the ship. God's creation being used in its limitless form!

As darkness falls, a sense of trepidation grows in the knowledge that without light the true nature of the world outside with all its beauty and hazards cannot be seen with the naked eye. A realisation of vulnerability dawns. What dangers lurk ahead? An unlit vessel? A submerged container floating just beneath the surface of the sea, undetectable until the ship's bow collides with it? An uncharted rock? In the darkness we rely on other senses and sensors to help us to navigate our way along: hearing, radar, sonar, night vision aids. But whilst these may detect an obstruction or the presence of something, they will not necessarily enlighten us to the nature of the object detected. We therefore sail on in faith, waiting for the dawn to appear and the sun to rise once more.

The Watchman forgoes his sleep to keep guard – if we are not watchful, we can be lulled into complacency leading us to miss the hazards before us and court disaster. Similarly, with our spiritual lives. We can become spiritually complacent putting ourselves on autopilot and not watching out for those daily hazards that can trip us up. Just as the lookout on the bridge needs to constantly scan the horizon, so too we need to scan our spiritual horizon.

The cycle of sunrise, daylight, sunset, darkness, is reminiscent of the life of Christ. The sun rises with his birth and sets with his death leaving us in darkness until he rises again in the resurrection of the new day. In the darkness we feel lost, vulnerable, uncertain, afraid. We are reliant on our faith to see us through the darkness in the expectation of Christ's second coming.

Advent is a time of anticipation, a time to wake up and start again. As the sun sets on the Church's old year, we need to take a bearing to check our spiritual compass and to check our spiritual position in the dusk that follows. Are we still on track, or have we allowed ourselves to drift, to be swept off course by sinful influences?

When the ship's Watchman spots the lights of another vessel, he assesses the likelihood of a collision. Are the lights on a steady bearing? If so, then a collision is inevitable and avoiding action such as a change of course or speed must be taken to prevent a catastrophe. How does he know to do this? He has learnt through training and experience, through good preparation, and by listening to his teachers and more experienced mentors. He has regularly practised his skill until he is proficient in dealing with unfamiliar and complex scenarios. To maintain that proficiency, the Watchman needs to regularly practise his skill and test himself in new situations.

In our Christian lives we too need to constantly practise our faith and test ourselves in unfamiliar waters. Advent provides an opportunity to switch off the autopilot and take control of our own personal helm, to use the aids available to us – catechesis, bible study, homilies, retreats – to learn about our faith, to listen more reverently and keenly to God's word and to ponder over it – what is God, my mentor, saying to me? What do I need to do to get back on my spiritual track?

As dawn begins to break, the Navigator, sextant in hand, "takes morning stars" and calculates the ship's position. Has the course correction made last night put us back on track? Are we now in the right place to start the activities of a new day?

Ian Crabtree, a retired Royal Navy Warfare Officer, is currently employed as the Pastoral Assistant to the Royal Navy Roman Catholic Chaplaincy. A husband, father and grandfather, he is a Knight of the Pontifical Order of St Gregory the Great (KSG).

Previously published in Advent Extra 2021

LOOK AT THE STARS

As a professional astronomer, Br Guy Consolmagno SJ spends his life stargazing. He reminds us that Advent is about looking at the stars and finding, not darkness, but the Light of the world.

When people think of astronomy and Advent, the Star of Bethlehem gets all the attention. In the days before Christmas of 2020 there was a conjunction of the planets Jupiter and Saturn that drew all sorts of attention to the perennial question of what the star might have been. While it was great fun watching the two bright planets night after night slowly advance together, this was not some totally unique event: such close conjunctions happen every few hundred years. And it was no cosmic sign; no one is expecting a new saviour's birth. That has already happened.

Indeed, all this attention on trying to suss out the Bethlehem Star is misleading on a number of accounts. After all, the important centre of the story should not be the nature of the star, any more than we should wonder about where the Wise Men got that gold or bought the frankincense. The centre of the story is not the star, but the Child.

It also has the unfortunate side effect of turning the Star into just a story, about another place and another time. But stars are really over our heads every night, visible from anywhere. And they too can lead us to Christ. It's not by doing calculations, like astrologers trying to use stars to control the future. We can find Christ by immersing ourselves into the larger, beautiful universe.

I'm a professional astronomer, and I have no problem with doing those calculations. That too can be a form of worship. Studying the cosmos in detail, like professionals and dedicated amateurs do, can add to the depth of how we immerse ourselves, just as the study of theology can bring a richness to our life of worship. But theology is different from prayer, and stargazing different from astronomy. Not everyone can be an astronomer; but anyone can sit under the sky and contemplate our place in the universe.

The stars exist. You can see them for yourselves, if you but take the time to look.

The stars are physical reminders that creation is so much larger than our day to day worries. From space you can look down on our planet and no longer see the turmoil which so many people have faced since the onset of Covid-19. But even without a worldwide pandemic, each of us individually live lives filled with individual crises that disrupt the way we'd gotten used to living. Look up towards the stars, though, and you'll see things in a larger perspective. They are the same stars that Galileo saw; that Shakespeare saw; that Christ saw overhead. They were there when we were children. They'll still be there, tomorrow.

The stars remind us that the entire universe is beautiful. There is beauty everywhere we look, if we but take the time to seek it. When God created the universe, he saw that it was good. And we are a part of that good universe. No matter how hard we try to mess things up, nothing that we human beings can do will change that! Indeed, Christ came precisely because God so loved the universe that He sent his Son to redeem it, to redeem us.

The stars show us a universe so large that we are sometimes afraid we'll be lost within it. But God, its creator, is even larger. Psalm 8 reminds us that God can find each of us and make us greater than angels.

But the stars also warn us of what we can lose if we're not careful. Just consider how we have blinded our night vision with harsh streetlights and garish neon. Pope Benedict once commented that this is a perfect analogy to human sin: filling the skies with our own lights to blot out the faint but beautiful lights God has placed above us.

Like the stars, God is always with us. But we need dark skies to see the stars. Advent is the time of year when we recall a universe before Christ's coming, a world that was both dark but filled with the whispers of a promise that the darkness would not last forever. Only in that darkness can we savour the light. Only in that anticipation can we embrace the joy of Christmas morning. Every child looking forward to opening presents knows that feeling; it is a sweet taste that we should recall from our childhoods, and never forget.

Advent is about looking at the stars and finding, not darkness, but the Light of the world.

Br Guy Consolmagno SJ is a Jesuit brother and astronomer, director of the Vatican Observatory and president of the Vatican Observatory Foundation.

Previously published in Advent Extra 2021

At the end, we will find ourselves face to face with the infinite beauty of God, and be able to read with admiration and happiness the mystery of the universe, which with us will share in unending plenitude…

In the meantime, we come together to take charge of this home which has been entrusted to us… Let us sing as we go. May our struggles and our concern for this planet never take away the joy of our hope.

God, who calls us to generous commitment and to give him our all, offers us the light and the strength needed to continue on our way. In the heart of this world, the Lord of life, who loves us so much, is always present. He does not abandon us, he does not leave us alone, for he has united himself definitively to our earth, and his love constantly impels us to find new ways forward. Praise be to him!

Laudato Si': on care for our common home: 243-245, 2015, Pope Francis

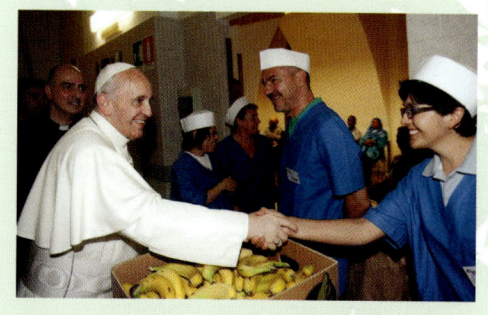

Pope Francis with Syrian refugees, © Jesuit Refugee Service

THE CANTICLE OF THE CREATURES

St Francis of Assisi

Most High, all powerful, good Lord, yours are the praises, the glory, the honour and all blessing.

To you alone, Most High, do they belong and no human is worthy to mention your name.

Praised be you, my Lord, with all your creatures, especially Sir Brother Sun, who is the day and through whom you give us light. And he is beautiful and radiant with great splendour; and bears a likeness of you, Most High One.

Praised be you, my Lord, through Sister Moon and the stars: in heaven you formed them clear and precious and beautiful.

Praised be you, my Lord, through Brother Wind; and through the air, cloudy and serene, and every kind of weather, through which you give sustenance to your creatures.

Praised be you, my Lord, through Sister Water, who is very useful and humble and precious and chaste.

Praised be you, my Lord, through Brother Fire, through whom you light the night: and he is beautiful and playful and robust and strong.

Praised be you, my Lord, through our Sister, Mother Earth, who sustains and governs us and who produces various fruit with coloured flowers and herbs.

Praised be you, my Lord, through those who give pardon for your love and bear infirmity and tribulation. Blessed are those who endure in peace: for by you, Most High, shall they be crowned.

Praised be you, my Lord, for our Sister, Bodily Death, from whom no one living can escape: woe to those who die in mortal sin.

Blessed are those whom death will find in your most holy will, for the second death shall do them no harm.

Published by
Redemptorist Publications

Wolf's Lane, Chawton, Hampshire,
GU34 3HQ, UK

www.rpbooks.co.uk

Tel. +44 (0)1420 88222
Email customercare@rpbooks.co.uk

A registered charity limited by guarantee

Registered in England 03261721

Copyright © Redemptorist Publications 2025

Remembering Francis: Champion of the Environment
Text compiled by Sr Janet Fearns
Design: Emma Repetti
Cover image: Pope Francis, St Peters Square, Vatican City, Riccardo Perna/Shutterstock.com
Images: Statue of Saint Francis of Assisi, Sibenik, Croatia, Alex Linch/Shutterstock.com; Pope Francis, St Peters Basilica, Vatican City, Fabrizio Maffei/Shutterstock.com; ©Sr Janet Fearns; with thanks to the Jesuit Refugee Service for permission to use their photographs.

Pages 11-154 previously Published as
Two Champions of the Environment (eBook)
Original Design: Eliana Thompson

ISBN 978-0-85231-576-7

All rights reserved. No part of this publication may be reproduced, stored in a retrieval system, or transmitted in any form or by any means, electronic, mechanical, photocopying, recording or otherwise, without prior permission in writing from Redemptorist Publications.

The moral right of the author to be identified as the author of this work has been asserted in accordance with the Copyright, Designs and Patents Act 1988.

A CIP catalogue record for this book is available from the British Library.

Printed by Short Run Press Ltd, Exeter